50
Social Emotional
Learning Lessons

Vol. I

DAVID PARIS

CONTENTS

5 STEPS
FOR SOCIAL EMOTIONAL MASTERY

Step 1. Read this book!

Step 2. Supplement this book with the SELAcademy and more at *BrooklySEL.com*.

Step 3. Schedule a free 15 minute consultation by emailing me at *info@BrooklynSEL.com*.

Step 4. Join the BrooklynSEL Facebook group.

Step 5. Bring BrooklynSEL to your school! We do in-person and virtual professional development for teachers, lead tier 1 restorative practices and offer an SEL show for kids with acrobats from America's Got Talent finalists.

For more information, go to
BrooklynSEL.com

IMAGINE

- Imagine a school where every student's social and emotional need is met so that academics can flourish.

- Imagine an emotional literacy curriculum that transforms students' relationships to their feelings through self-reflection, self-regulation, and responsible decision making.

- Imagine a classroom where personal sharing leads to belonging, respect, and inclusion for all students.

- Imagine a reduction of conflict through communication skills, active listening, and perspective taking.

- Imagine a culture of integrity that permeates every interaction in a community.

- Imagine students collectively excited about life.

This is possible...

https://vimeo.com/275941803

50 Social Emotional Lessons Vol. 1 will show you how to get there.

PREFACE

In the summer of 2018, the New York City mayor, the Police Commissioner, and the NYC Schools Chancellor came to Middle School 88 for a press conference celebrating our school's SEL (social emotional learning) environment as well as our reduction in school suspensions.

As the SEL Director at my school, my contribution to our school's success took many forms. I held community building circles with over 200 students weekly. I led professional development workshops teaching emotional literacy and our school's core values: respect, empathy, curiosity, integrity, and resilience. I facilitated restorative justice gatherings and mediated student conflicts. Additionally, I led meetings with classes that struggled with peer relationships and academic performance. I called these meetings a "Respect Reset" and they completely changed the trajectory of a class in just 45 minutes. This is what I did during the meetings:

- INCLUSIVE CIRCLE SEATING: I started the class by moving all the chairs into a circle so that everyone could see each other.

- GROUP AGREEMENTS: I proposed a set of agreements and asked for consensus.

- PERSONAL VALUE SHARE: We did a "Go around" where each person in the circle shared a value that was important to them. By doing this, everyone was seen and heard.

- GAME TO BUILD FUN & HOPE: The next step was to lead a fun, experiential game to enliven students and build hope that their classroom experience can be different.

- GAME REFLECTION: We reflected on what values were demonstrated during the game and how we could apply that knowledge to improve the class culture.

- CLASS ASSESSMENT ON WHAT IS GOING WELL: I posed two questions to the class for the next "Go around."
    1. What is going well in the class?
    2. What needs to be improved?

- VALIDATION & DISCUSSION ON IMPROVEMENTS: I facilitated a discussion about how to improve the culture in the class. I paraphrased every idea so that everyone's voice was validated.

- GROUP CONSENSUS ON NEXT STEPS: Based on what I heard from the class, I offered suggestions for actions to take and sought consensus from the group about what they wanted to do.

- APPRECIATION CLOSING: Lastly, I led a closing "Go around" where everyone shared something they liked or appreciated.

The "Respect Reset" works every time. Why?
- Student knowledge and experience is validated.

- Students are actively participating.

- Students draw upon their own experiential knowledge.

- Questions guide deep reflection.

- Connection is created.

- Hope is generated.

- Students feel a sense of agency for improving their class culture.

After the end of every "Respect Reset" meeting, students expressed their gratitude and desire for more opportunity to do this type of work. They wanted to be heard, they wanted to practice being with each other in a supportive environment, and they wanted skills to improve their social and emotional lives. Teachers expressed to me that they would love to lead this type of work, but they didn't know how to do it. And so I embarked on writing this book with the hope that every student will have an opportunity to learn social and emotional skills, create socially and emotionally safe classrooms, and teach students the skills they need to navigate a complex and challenging world.

INTRODUCTION

50 Social Emotional Learning Lessons is a comprehensive curriculum that teaches crucial skills at a pivotal time in our society. This book synthesizes the best practices of personal development, life coaching, and mindfulness into a clear set of instructions for teachers. There are ten units of instruction that span a broad spectrum of essential SEL skills and values. Each unit is a self contained set of lessons that can be taught independently or sequentially as part of a year long curriculum. Every unit meets all of the Social Emotional Learning Standards created by CASEL.org.

UNIT 1 — COMMUNITY: lays the foundation for connection, trust, and belonging with powerful icebreakers and interpersonal sharing.

UNIT 2 — ACTIVE LISTENING: develops the skill and practice of becoming a good listener.

UNIT 3 — RESPECT: creates opportunities for treating each other well and valuing kindness.

UNIT 4 — EMOTIONAL LITERACY: comprehensively explores feelings through games and reflection.

UNIT 5 — EMPATHY: builds upon a student's emotional awareness by practicing how to have compassion for someone else's experience.

UNIT 6 — COMMUNICATION: provides new frameworks for dialogue, handling conflict, and being assertive.

UNIT 7 — INTEGRITY: explores the importance of responsibility, keeping your word, and the impact of your actions.

UNIT 8 — MINDFULNESS: looks practically at how being present and aware can spark personal transformation and consciousness.

UNIT 9 — GOALS: empowers students to achieve something they want in life.

UNIT 10 — RESILIENCE: establishes a new mindset for overcoming challenges and achieving success.

These units are a blueprint for Social Emotional Learning. Each lesson engages students with a question that embraces their social emotional knowledge and experience. A skill is taught through Socratic-based discussion and then integrated using real life scenarios and experiential games. At the end of each lesson, students process their experience through reflection and integrate important tools for improving their social and emotional life.

50 Social Emotional Learning Lessons will help students cultivate a connection to their mind and emotions, so that they make responsible decisions. Students will develop communication skills to advance their social awareness and improve relationships. Classrooms can become nurturing environments for intrapersonal and interpersonal development. A journey of transformation awaits, one lesson at a time.

FAQ

Q: What is Social Emotional Learning?

A: Collaborative for Academic, Social, and Emotional Learning (CASEL) describes SEL as "The process through which children and adults understand and manage emotions, set and achieve positive goals, feel and show empathy for others, establish and maintain positive relationships, and make responsible decisions." For more information, go to CASEL.org.

Q: Why implement Social Emotional Learning in schools?

A: 1. Students want it. They are asking for help to understand themselves, their peer relationships, and their world. They want to learn in emotionally safe classrooms, be seen, and be heard. They want guidance for their lives and support for their interests and goals.

2. Administrators want it. SEL programs have proven to increase academic achievement and reduce bullying.

3. Parents want it. They are asking for support for their children's emotional regulation, executive functioning, and decision-making.

4. Businesses want it for their future workers. Social and emotional skills are important elements of productivity and are crucial in today's collaborative work environments.

Q: What if I don't know how to teach SEL?

A: The book is designed for you. The lessons were created based on simplicity and effectiveness. You don't need to have previous knowledge or training. You will only be required to pose a few questions, facilitate a group activity for practice, and lead reflections on what was learned.

Q: What if I am not very emotional?

A: Share your discomfort with the students and lead the lessons anyway. They will respect your willingness to try teaching SEL despite your unease. Authenticity is crucial to leading SEL. And once you start teaching the lessons, they will have so much fun and experience so much value, your discomfort will not be an issue.

Q: Do students need to sit in a circle?

A: The circle is a democratic structure that allows every student to see each other and symbolically shares the power within the group. The first SEL moment in the class could be an exploration of how the class can work together to move the chairs into a circle and place the tables on the perimeter. Alternatively, you can have students just move chairs to the perimeter of the room into an imperfect circular structure. It's not absolutely necessary, but it does signify to students that they are transforming the space for a significant purpose.

Q: What if I don't have time to teach SEL?

A: You can do as little as 10–15 mins a week and it will make a difference.

Q: Can I modify the lessons?

A: Yes. Modify anything based on the needs and interests of your class. A deep question or powerful story can sometimes lead to an in-depth discussion that will last the entire class. These moments become experiences that students will remember forever.

Q: Why are there so many questions?

A: Questions allow students to play an active role in their learning. Student engagement increases when their experience and knowledge is valued.

Q: How important are reflections?

A: Reflections are crucial to extract the full value of the activity. When students think about their experience, it offers them an opportunity to integrate what happened during the games and extend the lessons to other parts of their lives.

Q: How long should the reflections be?

A: No longer than 5 minutes. I use Outward Bound's three questions for reflection:

　　1. What happened? (Share their experience).

　　2. So what? (Articulate why this was meaningful to them).

　　3. Now what? (How to apply the lesson to other parts of their life).

Q: Should students be graded?

A: It depends. For some classrooms, individual grades are antithetical to SEL. In other classrooms, grades create accountability, rewards participation, and provides quantitative feedback. When time is limited, have students grade themselves. If time allows, ask students to write about their experience.

Q: What is the role of homework in SEL?

A: Homework extends the lesson beyond the classroom. You can create accountability by asking students to share their homework verbally at the start of the next class or you can have them submit a written reflection.

16

UNIT 1: Community Building

▶ Creates relationships and trust through ice breakers, sharing, and storytelling

▶ Establishes a foundation for safety, positivity, and support

▶ Fosters social engagement and communication

▶ Ensures that all students are seen and heard

LESSON 1: Classroom Agreements

Lesson Overview:

Activities in this Lesson:	About These Activities:
Opening Question	Builds intimacy through sharing stories about students' names.
Tiny Teach	Helps students value their knowledge and appreciate a positive learning environment.
Group Agreements	Facilitates a democratic structure for creating classroom norms.
Are You Like This or Like That?	Invites students to share something a little more personal about who they are.

SEL Standards: Relationship Skills / Self-Awareness

SEL Objectives: Communication / Recognizing Personal Strengths

ACTIVITY 1: Opening Question

Time: 10–15 mins

Ask: "What is the story behind your name?"

  a. Students can share who they are named after.

  b. Students can share a story about how their parents came up with their name.

c. Students can share whether their name has personal meaning to them.

d. If students don't know a story behind their name, they can share the way a parent says their name when they are mad at them.

ACTIVITY 2: Tiny Teach

Time: 15 mins

Instructions:

1. Introduce the game "Tiny Teach."

2. Students will have two minutes to teach someone else in the class something that is easy to learn.

3. Give an example of teaching something that would be easy to learn, such as:

   a. Teach a few words in another language (but not the entire language), or

   b. Teach a dance move (but not an entire choreography), or

c. Teach a recipe (but not a whole cookbook), or

d. Teach a strategy for a video game (but not all of them).

4. Make sure everyone has something to teach. If a student seems stuck, ask them to teach something related to what they like to do. If they still don't know, ask them to teach a technique they use for getting something they want from a parent.

5. Have students pair up, introduce themselves, and give them two minutes each to teach something.

6. Repeat one or more times with a new student.

Reflections:
- What was it like to teach someone else?
- What did you learn about teaching?

Teacher Note: This game can be used at the beginning of the year before discussing classroom norms.

ACTIVITY 3: Group Agreements

Time: 10–15 mins

Instructions:
1. Ask, "What made "Tiny Teach" a positive learning experience?"

2. Ask, "What agreements can we make so that everyone can have a positive learning experience in the class all year?"

3. Write these agreements on a sheet of chart paper or on a white board.

4. Ask, "Which agreements can be consolidated?" Where possible, consolidate agreements.

5. Ask students to give a thumbs up or thumbs down for each agreement.

6. If any student gives a thumbs down, ask them to explain their reasoning and suggest what works better for them.

7. Facilitate a discussion until a consensus for a complete list of agreements is reached.

8. Write the new set of agreements on chart paper.

9. Have every student sign it.

Reflection: Which agreement is the most important to you and why?

ACTIVITY 4: Are You Like This or Like That?

Time: 10–15 mins

Instructions: 1. Divide the class into groups of 4–5 students.

2. Pose the question and have each member of the group answer and explain their choice.

Example Questions:

a. Are you more like the sun or the moon?

b. Are you more like a highway or side street?

c. Are you more like a tree or flower?

d. Are you more like a river or ocean?

e. Are you more like breakfast or dinner?

Reflection: Did the group maintain the classroom agreements in this activity?

Homework: Notice how the classroom agreements affect the learning environment of the class.

LESSON 2: Getting To Know Each Other

Lesson Overview:

Activities in this Lesson:	About These Activities:
Opening Question	Asks whether you would prefer going backward or forward in time.
Move Your Butt If…	Combines relationship building with musical chairs.
Who Wrote That	Creates suspense and mystery while challenging students to notice each other.
If I Were A	Uses a creative metaphor to express who we are.

SEL Standards: Relationship Skills / Self-Awareness

SEL Objectives: Social Engagement / Self-Perception

ACTIVITY 1: Opening Question

Time: 5 mins

Ask: "If you could travel backward or forward in time, when and where would you want to go?"

ACTIVITY 2: Move Your Butt If...

Time: 10–15 mins

Instructions:

1. Have just enough seats in a circle for everyone except one volunteer, who will stand in the middle.

2. The volunteer says, "Move your butt if..." and states something physical like, "You are wearing blue."

3. Any sitting student wearing blue must get up and find another seat anywhere within the circle, except the seat to their immediate left or right. The initial volunteer also needs to race to claim a seat.

4. Tell students to move quickly, but also with safety in mind.

5. The student who is left standing after all the seats were claimed announces the next statement: "Move your butt if…"

6. After a few rounds of physical criteria, introduce statements of…

    a. Preferences such as, "Move your butt if you like ice cream." or

    b. Experiences such as "Move your butt if you have been on a roller coaster."

Variations:

- You can play this game without competition by changing the instruction to "Stand up if…"

- You can have the person in the middle give the prompt, "Never have I ever…"

Reflections:

- What was it like to share a commonality with someone else?

- What was it like to be different from the group?

ACTIVITY 3: Who Wrote That?

Time: 15–20 mins

Supplies: Index cards

Instructions:

1. Give out an index card to each student.

2. Ask students to write an unusual experience, talent, or fact about themselves that they don't mind sharing.

3. Collect the index cards, mix them up, and give them back out so that everyone has a new card.

4. Ask students to question each other to find the original author.

5. When a student finds the original author, the author signs the card and gives it to the teacher.

6. Post all of the index cards on a bulletin board in the classroom.

Reflections:

• What was something interesting that you enjoyed sharing about yourself?

• What was something interesting you learned about other members of the class?

ACTIVITY 4: If I Were A...

Time: 5–10 mins

Instructions:

1. Divide the class into groups of 4–6 students.

2. Give students the prompt one at a time. Ask students to answer it and explain why.

   a. If I were a type of weather, I would be _____.

   b. If I were a kitchen appliance, I would be a _____.

   c. If I were an item in the closet, I would be a _____.

   d. If I were a tropical animal, I would be a _____.

   e. If I were a famous building, I would be the _____.

Variation: Play as a class.

Reflections:

- What were you able to share about yourself through the questions?

- Did anyone's answer surprise you?

Homework: Consider asking a follow up question to anything you've learned about another student.

LESSON 3: Learning About Who We Are

Lesson Overview:

Activities in this Lesson:	About These Activities:
Opening Question	Asks about your birth order in your family.
Human Treasure Hunt	Helps students get to know each other.
Tracing Who We Are	Uses an outline of our bodies as a way to share experiences.
Web of Stories	Increases the level of intimacy through storytelling.

SEL Standards: Relationship Skills

SEL Objectives: Social Engagement / Relationship Building

ACTIVITY 1: Opening Question

Time: 5 mins

Ask: "How many siblings do you have or are you an only child?"

ACTIVITY 2: Human Treasure Hunt

Time: 10–15 min

Instructions: 1. Photocopy and distribute the Human Scavenger Hunt Worksheet.

A full size version of this worksheet is available in the appendix.

HUMAN SCAVENGER HUNT!!!

Has a pet other than a dog or cat	ENJOYS DANCING	HAS THEIR OWN YOUTUBE CHANNEL	Has a name longer than 6 letters	Speaks another language
Is left-handed	**Favorite color is purple**	Loves Math	**Plays an instrument**	Likes vegetables
Enjoys cooking	Likes talking in front of groups	Has a birthday in the same month	USES SAME BRAND OF TOOTH-PASTE	LIKES THE SAME VIDEO GAME
Same taste in shoes	**Loves snow**	HAS BROKEN A BONE	Has won an award	**Exercises every day**
Walks to school	**Likes the same music you do**	Does not like pizza	Can make a scary face	Likes to repair things

2. Tell students that they will have 5 minutes to find someone who matches the descriptions in the boxes.

3. Once they find someone who matches the description, they ask that student to sign their name in the box.

4. One student can only sign one box on the worksheet.

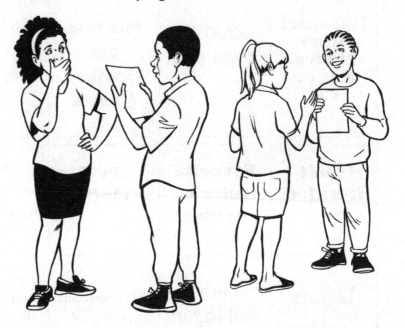

5. The goal is to have as many signatures as possible on the worksheet before time runs out.

Variations:

• Have multiple students sign their names in each box using their initials.

• Declare that the winner is anyone who has five boxes signed in a row.

• Have students create the content of the scavenger hunt based on what they want to know about other students. Everyone can have their own scavenger map, or the class can create one together.

Reflections:

• What did you learn about your classmates?

• What was it like to compete to get to know each other?

ACTIVITY 3: Tracing Who We Are

Time: 15–20 mins

Supplies: Copy paper

Instructions:

1. Draw an outline of a human on a marker board.

2. Share details about your life related to different parts of your body.

3. Write a sentence next to the corresponding body part.

   Example:

   a. "I saw the Grand Canyon"—near the eyes

   b. "I broke my arm"—near my elbow

c. "I love my dog"—near the heart

d. "I love spaghetti"—near the stomach

4. Give out a sheet of copy paper to teach students and have them create their own body outline.

5. When completed, have students leave their outlines on their table and do a gallery walk to see what other people created.

Reflection: What is something interesting that you learned about someone else in the class?

Teacher Note: Depending on the maturity of a class, it could be risky to use a full body outline. It's better to use just the top half of the body.

ACTIVITY 4: Web of Stories

Supplies: Ball of yarn (or string)

Instructions:

1. Hold a ball of yarn and tell a quick story about your life.

2. Ask anyone if they have a similar story or something your story makes them think about.

3. Whoever raises their hand, pass the ball of yarn to them as you hold one end of the yarn.

4. Have that student share their story or thoughts, and ask the rest of the class if what they shared reminds them of anything.

5. Keep passing the ball of yarn around until everyone has gotten a chance to share.

Reflection: How does the yarn reflect the connection people have with each other?

Homework: Now that you know more about your classmates, how has your experience in class changed?

LESSON 4: Group Values

Activities in this Lesson:	About These Activities:
Opening Question	Asks what you value most in life.
Individual Values	Offers an opportunity to share values through art and storytelling.
Sounds of the Universe	Is a popular team building game that demonstrates the joy in supporting each other.
Class Values	Is a democratic activity to discover what the class collectively finds important.

SEL Standards: Self-Awareness / Social Awareness

SEL Objectives: Self-Perception / Respect For Others

ACTIVITY 1: Opening Questions

Time: 5 mins

Ask:
1. "What value is most important to you?"

   Share examples like trust, family, creativity, connection, knowledge, friendship, love, justice.

2. "When have you experienced your value in your life?"

ACTIVITY 2: Individual Values

Time: 10–20 mins

Instructions: 1. Hand out 5″ x 7″ index cards and ask students to fold them in half.

                             a. On one side, have them write their names.

                             b. On the other side, have them write their values.

                             c. Have them decorate their cards, and on the inside, write a story about when they experienced their value.

                   2. Do a gallery walk so that students can view each other's cards.

Reflection: How did it feel to connect to your value?

34

ACTIVITY 3: Sounds of the Universe

Time: 5–10 mins

Instructions:

1. Ask for one volunteer to step out of the room.

2. Ask someone else to choose a spot in the room for the volunteer to find.

3. Ask for the volunteer to return to the room.

4. As the student enters the room, have students indicate how close or far the volunteer is to the spot by the intensity of their clapping of hands or thighs.

5. If the volunteer goes away from the spot, lessen the intensity.

6. If the volunteer goes towards the spot, increase the intensity.

7. Celebrate when the volunteer hits the spot.

8. Repeat!

Variations:

• Select two volunteers and divide the rest of the class into two groups. Assign each group a volunteer and compete over who can find the spot the fastest.

• Use facial expressions, but not sound, to guide volunteers.

- In addition to finding the spot, have the volunteer do a specific and easy-to-do task.

Reflections:
- What did it feel like to collectively help a classmate?
- What did it feel like to get support from the entire class?

ACTIVITY 4: Class Value

Time: 10–15 mins

Instructions:
1. Ask, "What did it feel like to collectively help a classmate?"
2. Ask, "What values were demonstrated in the activities?"
3. Ask the class to come to consensus for 5 values that will preserve the same energy for future lessons.
4. Write the values on the class agreements.

Reflection: Share one value that resonates with you after today's lesson and why it's important to you.

Homework: Notice when classmates support each other.

LESSON 5: Integrating Values

Lesson Overview:

Activities in this Lesson:	About These Activities:
Opening Question	Asks students to share an example of how the class values were actualized.
Group Juggling	Absorbs students in an engaging group challenge in order to practice class values.
Silent Line-up	Challenges students to create non-verbal solutions.
Acronym Party	Harnesses the power of group effort.

SEL Standards: Relationship Skills / Self-Awareness

SEL Objectives: Team Building

ACTIVITY 1: Opening Question

Time: 5 mins

Ask: "How have you seen or demonstrated the class values since the last time we met?"

ACTIVITY 2: Group Juggling

Time: 20–25 mins

Supplies: 20 Tennis balls or Koosh balls

Instructions:
1. Divide students into groups of 7–10 students and have them stand in a circle.
2. Explain that they will be juggling one or more tennis balls as a group.

3. Choose someone who will start the group juggle. That student will pass one ball underhanded to another student anywhere in the circle.

4. The student who receives the ball will then pass the ball to someone different in the circle.

5. Passes are always thrown to someone who has not yet received the ball.

6. This continues until everyone gets a chance to have the ball tossed to them.

   a. When possible, students should not pass the ball to someone next to them.

   b. If the ball drops, the group repeats the same passing pattern that was established when the first student tossed the ball to the second student.

   c. It is important to emphasize underhand tosses. If not, someone will mistake the activity for a professional baseball game.

7. When the ball reaches the last person, that student tosses the ball back to the first student.

8. Once everyone has touched the ball, the passing pattern has been established. Tell the class they will now repeat the established pattern, but ask them to try to do it a little faster.

9. After the group seems confident with this faster pattern, the group can now graduate to tossing two balls, one at a time. NOTE:

   a. They can keep adding balls into the group juggle every time they successfully complete the pattern without dropping a single ball.

   b. There is almost no limit to the number of balls that can be added.

Variations:
- Groups can add a verbal challenge such as saying the student's name when passing them the ball.

- Groups can reverse the passing pattern after they complete the first one.

- The group can simultaneously do the original passing pattern AND the reverse pattern using two balls.

- The circle can move clockwise or counterclockwise so students have to throw to a moving target.

Reflections:

- What can this activity teach us about how to support each other as a group?

- During an activity, what can you do to help someone else?

Teacher Notes:

- Demonstrate with a small group and show that when mistakes happen, the group can support each other.

- This is a great activity to check in midway and celebrate any positive displays of support. This support might mean giving information on how to catch, or how to toss a ball so someone can catch it more easily.

ACTIVITY 3: Silent Line-up

Time: 10–15 mins

Instructions:

1. Divide students into two groups of 10–15 students.
2. Explain that this activity is silent.
3. Tell students that they will have 4 minutes to line themselves up by the month and day of their birthday (not including year).

Variations:

- Restrict the techniques they use for success, such as:
  a. No mouthing words to each other,
  b. No writing,
  c. No using fingers to form letters or numbers.

- Have students line up alphabetically using their last name or their favorite animal.

Reflections:
- What strategies did you use?
- Were you surprised by the results?

ACTIVITY 4: Acronym Party

Time:
10–15 mins

Instructions:

1. Divide the class into groups of 4–6 students.

2. Define an acronym and give some examples:

   a. UFO = Unidentified Flying Object

   b. FBI = Federal Bureau of Investigations

   c. LOL = Laughing Out Loud

3. Give the class three letters of the alphabet.

4. Their task is to create their own acronyms with these three letters.

5. Let them know the acronyms have to make sense.

6. The group will have 2 minutes to brainstorm as many word combinations as possible.

7. After two minutes, tally the number from each group.

8. Repeat with a new set of letters.

Variation:
Use more than three letters.

Reflections:

• What was your process for creating acronyms?

• How did your group use teamwork?

Homework:
Notice when students act in agreement with the class values.

LESSON 6: Meaning

Lesson Overview:

Activities in this Lesson:	About These Activities:
Opening Question	Builds intimacy through sharing something meaningful about one's home.
Bin of Meaning	Asks students to share what's meaningful to them.
Community Mural	Visually creates meaning as a group.

SEL Standards: Relationship Skills / Self-Awareness

SEL Objectives: Relationship Building / Self Connection

ACTIVITY 1: Opening Question

Time: 5 mins

Ask: "What is your favorite spot at home or in your neighborhood and why?"

ACTIVITY 2: Bin of Meaning

Time: 10–15 mins

Supplies:
- Class set of index cards
- A small storage bin

Instructions:
1. Give out an index card to each student.
2. Ask students to write about an item that has meaning to them and why.

3. Give them the option of writing a story or drawing a picture.
4. After 5 minutes, have students place the index cards in the bin and give them the option of sharing what they wrote.
5. Keep the bin in the same location for future classes.

Reflections:
- How did you feel sharing what was meaningful for you?
- What was it like to hear about what was meaningful for others?

ACTIVITY 3: Community Mural

Time: 20–25 mins

Supplies:
- Chart paper
- Markers

Instructions:
1. Divide the class into 4 groups.
2. Give every group one sheet of chart paper and a collection of markers.
3. Have students choose one value that's important to them or assign a communal value to the class.
4. Tell students to write the value in large letters and decorate the paper with art, poetry, slogans, and uplifting imagery.
5. Have every student sign the chart paper and post it in the room or hallway.

Variation: Choose academic content as the subject matter of the mural.

Reflections:
- What were you able to contribute to the group?
- What are the advantages and disadvantages of doing art as a group?

Homework: Think about what rituals you have in your life that are meaningful to you.

UNIT 2: Active Listening

▶ Establishes what good listening looks / feels / sounds like

▶ Explores the roles of questions and responses while actively listening

▶ Utilizes paraphrasing as a tool for listening and understanding

▶ Teaches tools for respectful disagreement

LESSON 7: Listening Basics

Lesson Overview:

Activities in this Lesson:	About These Activities:
Opening Question	Asks students to think about what good listening skills looks like.
Looks / Sounds / Feels Like	Examines good and bad listening skills.
Concentric Circles	Uses the speed dating structure for quick interactions and listening practice.

SEL Standards: Relationship Skills

SEL Objectives: Listening Skills / Social Engagement

ACTIVITY 1: Opening Question

Time: 5 mins

Ask: "How do you know when someone is listening to you well or is not listening well?

ACTIVITY 2: Looks / Sounds / Feels Like

Time: 15–20 mins

48

Instructions:

1. Create the following chart:

Looks Like		Sounds Like		Feels Like	
😊	🙁	😊	🙁	😊	🙁

2. Ask two students to demonstrate listening skills in front of class.

3. Student A will answer your question and Student B will demonstrate good listening skills.

4. Give Student A the prompt, "What is the best invention? Why?"

5. After Student A answers, ask the class, "What did Student B look like when they demonstrated good skills." Emphasize the body actions (stillness, nodding head, eye contact).

6. Write the physical traits on the Looks Like T-chart under the happy face.

7. Give Student A a different question to answer and this time, Student B will do a poor job of listening.

8. Ask Student A, "What is the best gift you have ever received?"

9. After Student A answers the prompt, ask the class, "What did Student B look like when they showed poor listening skills?"

10. Fill out the chart under the sad face.

11. Divide the class into pairs. Repeat the process so everyone gets to experience good and poor listening skills.

12. Repeat the process to fill out the "Sounds Like" and "Feels Like" parts of the T-charts.

    Sample Questions:

    a. What are five things you want to achieve in your life?

    b. What is something you want to get better at?

13. Post the chart paper on the wall.

Reflection: What did you learn about good listening skills?

ACTIVITY 3: Concentric Circles

Time: 20–25 mins

Instructions:
1. Say, "Now that we know what good listening looks, sounds, and feels like, we are going to practice it."

2. Divide the class in half.

3. Have the group form two concentric circles: Group A is on the outside; Group B is on the inside.

4. Have the two groups face each other.

5. Group A will be the "talkers." Group B will be the "listeners."

6. Give Group A a prompt and give them 30 seconds to answer it.

7. Group B will listen and demonstrate good listening skills.

8. After 30 seconds, switch, Group B will answer the prompt, and Group A will listen.

9. Ask students to thank each other. Tell Group A to stand up and rotate one seat clockwise.

10. Repeat

Sample Questions:

  a. What's the best meal you have ever had?

  b. If you could be an expert in any subject, what would it be?

  c. How have you changed in the last five years?

  d. What is the best balance of life and work?

  e. What is the best job in the world? What's the worst?

Reflection: How do you feel after being listened to by so many of your peers?

Homework: Notice when you or others are listening well and when you and others are not.

LESSON 8: Open-ended Questions

Lesson Overview:

Activities in this Lesson:	About These Activities:
Opening Question	Asks students to consider who in their lives listens to them well.
Dog and Bone	Is a classic theater game created by Viola Spolin that makes being quiet essential and attunes our ear to all noises.
Asking Questions	Explores the importance of curiosity when listening to someone.
Walk and Talk	Transforms the classroom into a leisurely stroll with a friend, with whom you can discuss all life's topics.

SEL Standards: Relationship Skills

SEL Objectives: Listening Skills / Communication / Social Engagement

ACTIVITY 1: Opening Question

Time: 5 mins

Ask: "Who listens to you well?"

ACTIVITY 2: Dog and Bone

Time: 10–15 mins

Supplies: Any small object (a stuffed animal, book, ruler, or ball)

Instructions:

1. In the middle of a circle, a volunteer plays the role of a sleeping dog with his bone.

2. The dog lies down and must close their eyes.

3. Any object can be the bone and is placed in front of the dog, without any contact.

4. Choose one student, by pointing at them, whose job it will be to steal the bone.

5. If the dog hears a noise, the dog points in the direction of the bone thief.

6. If the dog correctly points at the culprit, congratulate the dog and the dog can open their eyes. The dog has the option of playing the dog in the next round.

7. If the dog points in the wrong direction, let the dog know that the point was unsuccessful and that the dog has two more tries.

8. If the bone thief successfully steals the bone and sits down without being pointed at, the round ends and the bone thief gets a roaring round of applause.

Variations:
- Have two bone thieves compete against each other.
- Have two dogs protect the bone.
- Have two bones.

Reflections:
- What techniques did the bone thieves use to stay quiet?
- What did you learn about listening?

Teacher Notes:
- Remind students that if they are not the bone thief, they must be completely quiet and still so as not to distract the dog.
- If a student does not want to lie on the floor, give them the option to sit in a chair.

ACTIVITY 3: Asking Questions

Time: 5–10 mins

1. Say, "Today, we are going to focus on another aspect of being a good listener: asking questions."

2. Ask, "What type of questions do you appreciate when you talk?"

3. Ask, "What type of questions do you ask to keep a conversation going?"

4. Ask, "How do you create interesting questions?"

5. Ask for two students to demonstrate listening and asking questions.

6. Student A will answer a prompt; Student B will ask them follow-up questions.

7. Divide students into pairs.

8. Have Student A answer a prompt and have student B ask Student A questions.

9. Switch roles:

Sample Prompts:

a. If your life was a movie with a soundtrack, what music would you use?

b. If you could blast different music throughout the day without anyone complaining, what songs would you choose?

c. If you could design a float for a parade, what would you make and who would you have on the float?

d. If you had to spend a week as one type of plant, what plant would you be?

e. Imagine you can create any one law; what would you create?

Reflection: How does asking questions affect a conversation?

ACTIVITY 4: Walk and Talk

Time: 15–20 mins

Instructions: 1. Establish a circular pathway for walking around the room.

2. Demonstrate a slow walking pace.

3. Pose a question.

a. What was your worst day ever? Your best day?

b. What is the best and worst advice you have ever heard? What is the best and worst advice you have ever given?

c. If you could have any three guests for a podcast or talk show, who would you choose?

d. If you could relive any time in your life, which time would you choose? Why?

e. What is one piece of advice you would give others based on your life experience?

4. Have students find a student they don't know very well and ask them to walk slowly on the pathway together.

5. Have students share their answers and ask each other follow up questions.

6. When they are finished, ask them to sit down. Have students:

   a. write down their partner's name.

   b. write down what their partner said.

   c. write down their follow up question.

7. After writing down their response, ask students to stand up and look for another person to walk and talk with.

Reflection: What did you learn about the relationship between good listening and asking questions?

Homework: Practice asking questions when listening to someone.

LESSON 9: Listening Responses

SEL Standards: Relationship Skills / Social Awareness

SEL Objectives: Listening Skills / Communication / Social Engagement

ACTIVITY 1: Opening Question

Time: 5 mins

Ask: "How do you like people to respond after you say something?"

ACTIVITY 2: The Art of the Response

Time: 20 mins

Instructions:

1. Ask, "Besides asking questions, how else can you respond that demonstrates good listening?"

2. List answers from the students (echoing words, giving feedback on what they say, sharing a similar experience, sharing agreement, sharing what makes sense, asking about what doesn't make sense).

3. Ask, "How do you know how to respond?"

4. Say, "Knowing how to respond is not a science: it's an art. Listen to your own mind about how to respond. With practice and reflection, you will become a master."

5. Divide the class into pairs.

6. Share a prompt and have students practice listening, asking questions, and responding.

   Sample Prompts:

   a. What was your favorite present that you ever gave or received?

   b. What art form interests or inspires you and why?

   c. What was the longest day of your life, and why?

   d. Where is the most interesting place you have visited and why?

   e. When are you happiest and why?

Reflection: What is your favorite response when someone is listening to you?

ACTIVITY 3: Group Conversations

Time: 20 mins

Instructions:

1. Ask, "How does listening in a group differ from listening to just one person?"

2. Ask, "What do you have to do to listen and respond well in a group conversation?"

3. List responses on the marker board or chart paper.

4. Say, "We are going to practice what it means to listen well in a group."

5. Divide the class into groups of 4–5 students.

6. Give the students / groups a statement to discuss:

   Sample Statements:

   a. Playing a game is fun only when you win.

   b. Decisions that people make quickly are always wrong.

   c. Luck has nothing to do with success.

   d. It's okay to lie.

   e. Exams are the best way to motivate students.

Reflection: What did you learn about responding and listening?

Homework: Notice how you and others respond that demonstrates poor or good listening skills.

LESSON 10: Paraphrasing

Lesson Overview:

Activities in this Lesson:	About These Activities:
Opening Question	Explores what problems occur when there is miscommunication.
Back to Back Drawing	Brings awareness to language and the need to be precise.
Paraphrase Practice	Introduces a powerful tool for demonstrating understanding.
Communication Breakdown	Illustrates the value of paraphrasing.

SEL Standards: Relationship Skills / Social Awareness

SEL Objectives: Communication / Perspective-Taking

ACTIVITY 1: Opening Question

Time: 5 mins

Ask: "When has miscommunication been a problem in your life?"

ACTIVITY 2: Back to Back Drawing

Time: 10–15 mins

Supplies: Blank paper

Instructions:

1. Divide the class into pairs.

2. Have students sit or stand back to back.

3. Student A will draw a simple picture with at least 2 geographic shapes in 30 sec.

4. Give students a few example pictures, so they know this exercise is not an art competition.

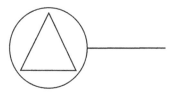

5. Student A has 2 minutes to describe how to draw their picture. Student B listens, is not allowed to talk, and does their best job to replicate the picture.

6. Compare the pictures.

7. Switch roles and repeat the process.

8. Repeat activity with the same partner or a new partner.

Variations:
- You can give out preset drawings for students to describe.
- One person describes the drawing to a group of 3–4 students.
- Add more time to make the drawings more complex.
- Play a second round and allow Student B to ask questions.
- Instead of drawings, use blocks, Legos, or craft materials.

Reflections:
- Did your drawings look like what was described?
- What was difficult about describing the image? About listening?
- What did you learn about communication?

ACTIVITY 3: Paraphrase Practice

Time: 10–15 mins

Instructions:
1. Ask, "Are you surprised when what a person heard differs from what you said?"

2. Say, "To increase our communication skills we are going to practice "Paraphrasing.' Paraphrasing is expressing what someone said in your own words."

3. Demonstrate paraphrasing by asking a student questions and expressing what they say in your own words.

4. Ask the student if you understood them correctly by asking, "Is that right?"

5. Explain verifying accuracy after paraphrasing is crucial. If the paraphrase was inaccurate, the speaker can clarify their meaning.

6. Divide students into pairs.

7. Ask Student A to answer a question and Student B to paraphrase what they heard. Then switch roles.

   Sample Questions:

   a. If you were an animal, which one would you be and why?

   b. Why do we sometimes have to stop and think before talking?

   c. If you could be an expert in two subjects, what would they be and why?

Reflection: How did paraphrasing improve communication?

ACTIVITY 4: Communication Breakdown

Time: 15–20 mins

Instructions:
1. Ask for five students to leave the room.

2. Choose a student in the class, Student A, to tell a three or four sentence story.

3. Ask for one student, Student B, to return from outside the room.

4. Have Student A share their story with Student B.

5. Student B asks for Student C to come in from outside the classroom.

6. In front of the class, Student B shares Student A's story with Student C.

7. Student C asks for Student D to come in from outside of the classroom.

8. Student C then shares what he or she heard to student D.

9. Repeat until the story is shared five times.

10. Play again, but allow the listener to paraphrase and ask whether they got the story right.

Reflection: How does paraphrasing help communication?

Homework: Paraphrase what someone says to make sure you understand them.

LESSON 11: Paraphrasing with Tone

Lesson Overview:

Activities in this Lesson:	About These Activities:
Opening Question	Asks students to consider the importance of tone.
Blah, Blah, Blah	Introduces the importance of listening to someone else's tone.
Paraphrase Practice With Tone	Offers the opportunity to practice an advanced form of paraphrasing.

SEL Standards: Relationship Skills

SEL Objectives: Communication / Perspective-Taking

ACTIVITY 1: Opening Question

Time: 5 mins

Ask: "What tone of voice gets your attention?"

ACTIVITY 2: Blah, Blah, Blah

Time: 15 mins

Instructions:
1. Divide students into pairs.

2. Assign all students with a character, setting, and conflict. Use examples such as:

   a. Two friends find a wallet on the street. One friend wants to keep it, the other friend wants to find the rightful owner.

BLAH, BLAH, BLAH.

        b. A customer is upset with the waiter at a restaurant because the soup is cold.

        c. A parent tries to fix a child's shirt for a photo, but the child doesn't want to be bothered.

3. Within those parameters, the two students engage in a conversation using only the word "blah," using tone and nonverbal communication to convey meaning.

Variations:

- Only tell Student A the Who, What, Where. After a "blah" conversation, have Student B guess the Who, What, and Where.

- Try the same activity without any words, not even using "blah."

- Try the same activity without any movement, just "blah" and tone.

Reflections:

- What were you able and unable to communicate?

- How did your physicality and tone affect comprehension?

ACTIVITY 3: Paraphrase Practice With Tone

Time: 25 mins

Instructions:

1. Say, "We are going to combine our awareness of tone with paraphrasing.

2. Demonstrate paraphrasing with a student. Communicate not only what you heard, but also match the tone with a student. After paraphrasing, ask the student, "Is that right?"

3. Ask a student, "What is the most disgusting thing you ever had to eat?"

4. Divide the students into two groups and have them face each other for concentric circles.

5. Tell Group A that they will be the "talkers" and Group B will paraphrase what they hear with tone in mind.

6. After Group A answers a prompt and Group B paraphrases, have the pairs switch roles.

Sample Questions:

a. "What is your favorite family recipe or favorite dessert?"

b. "How do you feel when someone accuses you of something you didn't do?"

c. "What is something you have done that you are proud of?"

d. "What is something you have done that you are not proud of?"

7. Ask students to thank each other.

8. Tell Group A to stand up and rotate one seat clockwise.

9. Repeat.

<u>Variations:</u>	How did listening to tone affect your feeling of being heard?
<u>Homework:</u>	Practice paraphrasing while matching someone's tone.

LESSON 12: Listening and Disagreement

Lesson Overview:

Activities in this Lesson:	About These Activities:
Opening Question	Introduces the topic of disagreement.
Sharing Understanding in Disagreement	Tests the student's ability to paraphrase what they hear.
Logical Understanding	Asks students to state the logic of someone else's opinion.

SEL Standards: Relationship Skills

SEL Objectives: Perspective-Taking

ACTIVITY 1: Opening Question

Time: 5 mins

Ask: "What do you do when you disagree with someone?"

ACTIVITY 2: Sharing Understanding In Disagreement

Time: 20–25 mins

Instructions:

1. Ask, "How can you listen well but disagree with someone?" (Use a non-confrontational tone, state that you are giving your opinion, acknowledge that you hear what they are saying).

2. Say, "One way to demonstrate listening well while disagreeing is to paraphrase what you hear them say first. When people feel heard first, they are more likely to hear what you have to say. We are going to practice this skill while discussing some controversial topics. For this activity, before you share your opinion, you must paraphrase what you heard the other person said first."

3. Introduce the first topic: "Is water wet?"

4. Call on the first student to raise their hand. When Student A finishes sharing their argument, as, Student A to call on someone else, make sure to remind them to paraphrase what they heard first.

Other topics include:

a. "Is cereal a soup?"

b. "Is the thumb a finger?"

c. "If you clean out a vacuum cleaner, are you a vacuum cleaner?"

Variation:	Have students debate preferences such as mountains or oceans, cats or dogs, night or day.
Reflections:	• Were you able to communicate your perspective?
	• Did you understand the arguments of anyone who disagreed with you?

ACTIVITY 3: Logical Understanding

Time:	15–20 mins
Instructions:	1. Say, "Another way to demonstrate listening well while disagreeing is to explain why someone else's argument makes logical sense."
	2. Demonstrate with a student.
	For example, if a student argues that, "Water can't be wet because it's water," you might say, "That makes sense that water is not wet because water can't be on water. Is that right?" And then give your opinion.
	3. Continue with a new debate topic. Have students first explain why someone else's argument makes sense before disagreeing with it.
	Sample Topics:
	a. Life is easier for children now than fifty years ago.
	b. People behave differently when they wear different clothes.
	c. Never ever give up.
	d. Technology has made the world a better place to live.
	e. Watching television is bad for children.
Reflection:	How did paraphrasing and acknowledging the logic of someone's argument affect the discussions?
Homework:	Practice disagreeing agreeably.

UNIT 3: Respect

▶ Demonstrates the value of respect in a classroom

▶ Practices treating people the way they want to be treated

▶ Promotes inclusion

▶ Facilitates random acts of kindness

LESSON 13: All About Respect

Lesson Overview:

Activities in this Lesson:	About These Activities:
Opening Question	Introduces the topic of respect.
Shared Definition	Creates dialogue around what respect means.
Group Knot	Provides an opportunity to practice respect in a group activity.

SEL Standards: Social Awareness / Relationship Skills

SEL Objectives: Respect for Others / Teamwork

ACTIVITY 1: Opening Questions

Time: 5 mins

Ask:
1. "What does respect mean to you?"
2. "How do you know when someone is giving you respect or not?"

ACTIVITY 2: Shared definition

Time: 20 mins

Supplies:
- 30 sheets of paper
- markers

Set up:
- Search the internet for quotes about respect and write them on the sheets of paper.
- Spread the respect quotes around the room.

Instructions:
1. Ask students to walk around the room and choose one quote about respect.
2. Divide the class into groups of 5-6 students.
3. Ask students to share why they chose their quote to the group.
4. Ask each group to come up with a shared definition of respect in 5 minutes.
5. Ask each group to designate one person to share this definition with the class.

Reflection:
How did your understanding of respect change after your group discussion?

ACTIVITY 3: Group Knot

Time: 20 mins

Instructions:
1. Say, "We are going to do a group challenge. As your group tries to accomplish this task, notice how respect plays a role in the group's success."

2. Divide the students into groups of 7–9 students.

3. Have students stand in a circle shoulder-to-shoulder.

4. Have each person put both of their hands into the center of the circle.

5. Grab a hand from two different people and not anyone next to you.

6. The challenge is to become "untangled" without letting go. (You can allow students to rotate their hands when they get stuck, but not let go.)

7. The group usually ends up in a large circle, but sometimes two circles can form.

8. Ask, "How did you demonstrate respect in this activity?"

Reflection: How did students demonstrate respect during the activities?

Homework: Notice at least one act of respect.

LESSON 14: Treating Others with Respect

Lesson Overview:

Activities in this Lesson:	About These Activities:
Opening Question	Considers what respect looks like.
Two Golden Rules	Proposes an advanced version of the Golden Rule.
Creator, Sculptor, Clay	Gives students the experience of how respect can be reciprocated.

SEL Standards: Social Awareness / Relationship Skills

SEL Objectives: Respect for Others / Teamwork

ACTIVITY 1: Opening Questions

Time: 5 mins

Ask: 1. "How do you want others to demonstrate respect to you?"

2. "How do you demonstrate respect to others?"

ACTIVITY 2: Two Golden Rules

Time: 20 mins

Instructions:	1. Say, "The Golden Rule is do unto others as you wish them to do unto you."
	2. Ask, "How do you treat others? How do you wish they would treat you?"
	3. Ask, "Does the Golden Rule work in your life?"
	4. Say, "Another way to think of the Golden Rule is to treat others the way they want to be treated."
	5. Ask, "What works and what's challenging about this version of the rule?"
	6. Ask, "How do you know what someone else wants?"
	7. Tell students to turn and talk to someone about one person in their life and how that person likes to be treated.

Ask:

a. "Who in your life likes their own space and doesn't like anyone touching their stuff?"

b. "Who in your life doesn't like any sort of teasing?"

c. "Who in your life doesn't want anyone in their business."

Reflection: How can you use the "second" Golden Rule in your life?

ACTIVITY 3: Creator, Sculptor, Clay

Time: 20 mins

Instructions:
1. Divide the class into groups of 3 students.

2. Each student chooses a role—Creator, Sculptor, or Clay.

3. Explain that everyone will have a chance to do each role.

4. The Creator stands back-to-back with Clay.

5. The Creator creates a shape with their bodies that they can sustain for 1 minute.

6. The Sculptor tells the Clay how to move so they match the same position as the Creator.

7. After 1 minute, the Creator turns around and observes the Sculptor's work.

8. Everyone should switch roles and repeat until each person has tried each role.

Variations:
- Increase the difficulty by telling the Creator to move one or more limbs in a consistent pattern.

- You can increase group size to 5 students, with two Creators and two Clays.

Reflections:
- How was the "second" Golden Rule applied in this activity?

- How were people respectful of each other?

Homework: Notice the different ways people want to be respected.

LESSON 15: Inclusion

Lesson Overview:

Activities in this Lesson:	About These Activities:
Opening Question	Asks students to reflect about their experiences with inclusion and exclusion.
Commonalities and Differences	Examines how to be respectful of both the ways we are similar and different.
Jigsaw Puzzle	Is a physical and metaphorical way of coming together.

SEL Standards: Social Awareness / Relationship Skills

SEL Objectives: Respect for Others / Social Engagement

ACTIVITY 1: Opening Question

Time: 5 mins

Ask: "When have you ever felt included or excluded from a group?"

ACTIVITY 2: Commonalities and Differences

Time:

15 mins

Instructions:

1. Divide the class into 4 groups.

2. Have each group go to one corner of the room.

3. Tell each group to come up with a list of everything they have in common.

4. Encourage students to find unusual commonalities instead of obvious ones.

5. After five minutes, have each group share their most interesting commonalities with the class.

6. Ask, "What was it like to be included in some commonalities and excluded from others?"

7. Ask, "How did respect play a role in this activity?"

8. Tell each group to come up with a way everyone in the group is different.

9. After five minutes, have each group share their most interesting differences with the class.

10. Ask, "Did acknowledging differences affect respect in the group?"

11. Ask, "What are the benefits of respecting differences?"

Reflections:

- What was it like to learn commonalities among your classmates?

- What was it like when you struggled to find something in common with someone else?

- What was it like to identify the differences with your classmates?

Teacher Note:

Encourage students to find unusual commonalities instead of obvious ones.

ACTIVITY 3: Jigsaw Puzzle

Time: 25 mins

Supplies: 6 100-Piece jigsaw puzzles

Instructions:
1. Ask, "Why do groups sometimes exclude people?"

2. Ask, "How can we make people feel more included in class?"

3. Divide students into 6 groups.

4. Give students 20 minutes to complete the puzzle.

Variation: Students must complete the puzzle without speaking.

Reflection: How will inclusion strengthen our class?

Homework: Take one action towards inclusion. Notice how you feel.

LESSON 16: Kindness Experiment

Lesson Overview:

Activities in this Lesson:	About These Activities:
Opening Question	Introduces experiences of kindness.
Broken Squares	Constructs a scenario in which all members of a group need each other.
Why Kindness	Introduces the importance of being kind and its benefits.

SEL Standards: Social Awareness / Relationship Skills

SEL Objectives: Respect for Others / Teamwork

ACTIVITY 1: Opening Question

Time: 5 mins

Ask: "What's the nicest thing you have ever done for someone? What's the nicest thing someone did for you?"

ACTIVITY 2: Broken Squares

Time: 25–30 mins

Supplies:

- Poster board or cardboard
- Scissors
- 25 Large envelopes

Set up:

- Use the diagram in "Preparation for Broken Squares" to create 15 broken pieces of a square for each group.
- Label each envelope with one letter from A-E.
- Using the letters on the diagram, find the pieces that go to each envelope.

Preparation:

1. Cut five cardboard squares of equal size (six-by-six inches).
2. Mark each square as shown in the illustration.
3. The lines should be drawn so all pieces with the same shape will be exactly the same size.
4. After drawing the lines, cut each square into the smaller pieces that will make up the puzzle.
5. Mark five envelopes with the letters A, B, C, D, and E.
6. Distribute the puzzle pieces into their corresponding envelopes.

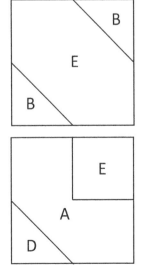
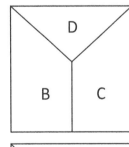
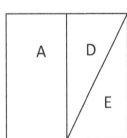
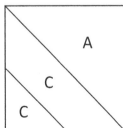

Instructions:

1. Divide the class into groups of five. If there are extra students, they can be observers or judges.

2. Each group gets five envelopes labeled A through E.

3. Explain that a square has been broken. Each group member has three pieces of the square.

4. Explain that the group's task is to put five equally sized squares back together.

5. Let them know that for this activity, they can not talk.

6. They also can not ask for anyone else's piece, verbally or non-verbally.

7. They may, however, give any number of pieces to a teammate as many times as they like.

Reflections:

- Was it challenging to need others in order to fix your broken square?

- How is this game a metaphor for life?

ACTIVITY 3: Why Kindness?

Time: 10–15 mins

Instructions:

1. Ask, "How can kindness benefit you?"

2. Show the YouTube video, "The Science of Kindness." *https://www.youtube.com/watch?v=O9UByLyOjBM&t=52s*

3. Ask, "What is the science behind being kind?"

4. Say, "Plan for acts of kindness in three areas of your life: friends, family and community."

5. Ask students to share their kindness plans.

Reflections:

• What did you notice about how you felt when you did something kind?

• What effect did it have on someone else?

Homework: Do three acts of kindness. How did you feel afterwards? What happened after you did something kind?

UNIT 4: Emotional Literacy

▶ Connects students to a universe of feelings

▶ Challenges students to identify feelings in others

▶ Investigates the role of feelings in decision making and actions

▶ Uses feelings to improve dialogue

LESSON 17: Connecting to Feelings – Part 1

Lesson Overview:

Activities in this Lesson:	About These Activities:
Opening Question	Asks students to connect to their feelings.
Notice Your Feelings	Helps students notice they are feeling something every moment of their lives.
Feelings Charades	Is a theatrical game for noticing someone else's feelings.
Feelings Scenarios	Helps students explore why they might be feeling a certain way.

SEL Standards: Self-Awareness

SEL Objectives: Identifying Emotions

ACTIVITY 1: Opening Question

Time: 5 mins

Ask: "What feelings have you had so far today?"

ACTIVITY 2: Noticing Your Feelings

Time: 10–15 mins

Supplies:
- Any small item you can put in a student's palm
- Paper and pen / pencil

Instructions:

1. Tell students this exercise trains us to notice our feelings.

2. Announce to the class: "Everyone is going to receive a gift."

3. Tell students to write down whatever they feel at the moment they hear this announcement. Give some examples of potential feelings: excitement, surprise, indifference, nervousness.

4. Tell students that to get the gift, they will have to put their elbows on their thighs and hold their palms out.

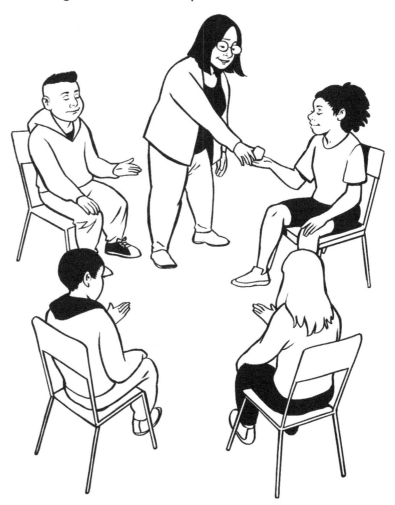

5. Ask them, "How do you feel?" and have them write their feelings down.

6. Tell them to close their eyes. Say, "You will now receive your gift, but you have to keep your eyes closed when you receive your gift."

7. Ask them, "How do you feel?" and have them write that down.

8. Tell them that for the next few feelings, their eyes will be closed, so they don't have to write them down.

9. Once every student has their eyes closed, ask them to notice what they are feeling.

10. Ask students to stay quiet as you walk around. Put one item in each students' hand.

11. Tell the students to close their hands and notice the texture of the gift, while noticing what they are feeling.

12. Tell students to open their hands and eyes and notice how they are feeling.

13. Have students turn and talk to their neighbor about what they experienced.

14. Ask students to complete the feelings list.

Variations:
- Do a second round and change the item.
- Give out a list of feelings beforehand.

Reflections:
- Did you feel something at all times? Feeling numb, indifferent, or bored is still a feeling.
- Did your feelings change from moment to moment?

Teacher Note:
At some point in this unit, a student will ask about the difference between feelings and emotions. This topic is a huge scholarly pursuit, but the distinction doesn't serve students at this point in their emotions / feeling literacy. For now, it's best to say that they are synonymous, but may require a subtle distinction in the future.

ACTIVITY 3: Feelings Charades

Time: 10–15 mins

Supplies: 80 index cards.

Set up: Write one feeling on each card.

Instructions:
1. Divide the class into four groups and have each group form a circle.

2. Place a deck of 20 feeling index cards each within the center of every circle.

3. Ask for a volunteer to go to the middle of the circle.

4. This volunteer will choose one feeling index card. Then they will make a pose that demonstrates that feeling.

5. The students in the circle will guess which emotion the volunteer is expressing.

6. This volunteer may not speak during their pose, but they will need to indicate whether a guess is correct or not.

7. Each student goes into the middle of the circle at least once.

8. After 5 minutes, have the groups rotate to a new set of feeling cards.

Variation: Have students add a monologue to their pose.

Reflections:
*   What nonverbal cues were you able to detect in order to make a feelings guess?

*   When and how is this skill useful in life?

ACTIVITY 4: Feelings Scenarios

Time: 5–10 mins

Instructions:

1. Keep students in the same group.

2. Tell students that you will be sharing different scenarios in life. Their task is to share with the group how they would feel in that scenario and why.

3. Announce different scenarios.

   Sample Scenarios:

   a. You are unprepared for a test.

   b. You wake up in the morning.

   c. Your cell phone is missing.

   d. You receive a compliment.

   e. You hear gossip.

   f. You are blamed for something you didn't do.

   g. You enter a room full of new people.

   h. You receive a gift.

   i. You give a gift.

   j. It's snowing outside.

Reflection: What did you learn about feelings today?

Homework: Notice your feelings.

LESSON 18: Connecting to Feelings — Part 2

Lesson Overview:

Activities in this Lesson:	About These Activities:
Opening Question	Reviews what they have been feeling recently.
Emotional Stacking	Categorizes feelings by intensity level.
Feelings Art	Uses a visual medium to integrate and express feelings.

SEL Standards: Self-Awareness

SEL Objectives: Identifying and Expressing Emotions

ACTIVITY 1: Opening Question

Time: 5 mins

Ask: "What was one feeling you felt between last class and this class?"

ACTIVITY 2: Emotional Stacking

Time:　　　　　20–25 mins

Instructions:
1. Say, "Now that we have identified different feelings, we are going to group them by category and emotional intensity."

2. Divide the class into groups of 4–5 students.

3. Give each group copies of the Emotional Stacking List.

   A full size version of this worksheet is available in the appendix.

☺ Feelings Associated with Met Needs ☺

Excited ➡ **Excited**	**Happy** ➡ **Happy**	**Hopeful** ➡ **Hopeful**
Energetic　1) _____	Blissful　1) _____	Confident　1) _____
Enthusiastic　2) _____	Delighted　2) _____	Expectant　2) _____
Passionate　3) _____	Joyful　3) _____	Light hearted 3) _____
Surprised　4) _____	Pleased　4) _____	Upbeat　4) _____

Inspired ➡ **Inspired**	**Interested** ➡ **Interested**	**Peaceful** ➡ **Peaceful**
Amazed　1) _____	Curious　1) _____	Refreshed　1) _____
Motivated　2) _____	Enchanted　2) _____	Relaxed　2) _____
Psyched　3) _____	Fascinated　3) _____	Relieved　3) _____
Stirred　4) _____	Intrigued　4) _____	Satisfied　4) _____

☹ Feelings Associated with Unmet Needs ☹

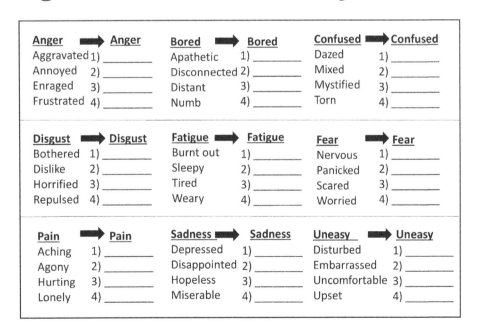

Anger ➡ **Anger**	**Bored** ➡ **Bored**	**Confused** ➡ **Confused**
Aggravated 1) _____	Apathetic　1) _____	Dazed　1) _____
Annoyed　2) _____	Disconnected 2) _____	Mixed　2) _____
Enraged　3) _____	Distant　3) _____	Mystified　3) _____
Frustrated 4) _____	Numb　4) _____	Torn　4) _____

Disgust ➡ **Disgust**	**Fatigue** ➡ **Fatigue**	**Fear** ➡ **Fear**
Bothered　1) _____	Burnt out　1) _____	Nervous　1) _____
Dislike　2) _____	Sleepy　2) _____	Panicked　2) _____
Horrified　3) _____	Tired　3) _____	Scared　3) _____
Repulsed　4) _____	Weary　4) _____	Worried　4) _____

Pain ➡ **Pain**	**Sadness** ➡ **Sadness**	**Uneasy** ➡ **Uneasy**
Aching　1) _____	Depressed　1) _____	Disturbed　1) _____
Agony　2) _____	Disappointed 2) _____	Embarrassed　2) _____
Hurting　3) _____	Hopeless　3) _____	Uncomfortable 3) _____
Lonely　4) _____	Miserable　4) _____	Upset　4) _____

4. Say, "As a group, decide which feelings belong in which category."

5. Say, "After you categorize them, stack them based on the intensity of the feeling. The most intense version of the feeling should be on the bottom and the least intense version should be on the top."

6. After 10 minutes, have the groups share their results with the class and discuss any differences.

7. Share a story in which the intensity of a feeling grew over time.

8. Ask if anyone in the class has a similar story.

Reflection: Why might it be useful to identify different levels of a feeling?

ACTIVITY 3: Feelings Art

Time: 15–20 mins

Instructions: 1. Ask students to choose one emotion or set of emotions and draw
                        a picture, share a story, or create a poem about that feeling.

                     2. After completing the art project, have students view each other's
                        work in a gallery walk.

Reflection: Which feelings did you connect with today?

Homework: Identify how your feelings either went up or down in intensity and why.

LESSON 19: Feelings Practice

Lesson Overview:

Activities in this Lesson:	About These Activities:
Opening Question	Asks to consider other people's feelings.
Group Feelings Search	Playfully approaches feelings by identifying what other people might be feeling.
Follow the Leader / Feelings Version	Is a playful variation of a traditional game using feelings.
Feelings in a Bag	Uses anonymity to share personal experiences with feelings.

SEL Standards: Self-Awareness / Relationship Skills

SEL Objectives: Identifying and Expressing Emotions / Social Engagement

ACTIVITY 1: Opening Question

Time: 5 mins

Ask: "How can you tell what someone is feeling?"

ACTIVITY 2: Group Feelings Search

Time: 5–10 mins

Supplies: Index cards

Instructions:

1. Use the same number of cards as there are students in your class.

2. Write one of seven feelings on the back of every card, with each feeling getting written at least three times.

   For example, if there were 28 students in a class, you could write joy on 6 cards, frustration on 5 cards, sadness on 5 cards, confusion on 3 cards, fear on 3 cards, relaxed on 3 cards, and energized on 3 cards.

3. Give a card to each student and explain that the card has an emotion to act out. Let students know they can not show their card to anyone.

4. Their task is to find who else has the same feeling card without talking.

5. When students think they have found everyone in their group, they stand next to each other.

6. Once everyone is in a group, have students reveal their emotions to each other to see if they are in the correct group.

Reflections:

- What cues did you give to indicate how you felt?

- What did you see in other students' expressions that indicated what they were feeling?

ACTIVITY 3: Follow the Leader / Feelings Version

Time: 15–20 mins

Instructions:

1. Have everyone gather in a circle.

2. Play the first round of Follow the Leader with traditional rules:

   a. Student A leaves the room.

   b. A leader is selected to set movements for the class.

   c. Everyone mimics what the leader does.

   d. When the leader changes movements, everyone follows, without making it obvious who the leader is.

   e. Student A comes back, stands in the center of the circle, and has three guesses to figure out who the leader is.

3. In the second round, the leader will add specific emotion to their movement. When the leader changes the movement, they must also change their emotional expression. Students must follow the leader physically and copy the same emotional expression.

4. In the third round, the class follows the leader's emotional state, but chooses their own individual movement. When the leader changes their emotional state, the other students must change to follow the new emotional state of their leader, while maintaining their original movement.

Reflections:

- Was it difficult to copy the leader's emotional state?

- Did acting out an emotion make you feel any differently?

ACTIVITY 4: Feeling in a bag

Time: 10–20 mins

Supplies: 150 strips of paper

Instructions:

1. Give out five strips of paper to each student.

2. Tell students the class will be sharing their emotional thoughts, questions, and experiences, starting with fear.

3. Tell students to write one thing they are afraid of on one of their strips of paper.

4. Let students know you will collect the strips in a bag and read the strips out loud anonymously.

5. Give a minute for students to write their fear and then collect the strips.

6. Choose a few strips to read out loud and facilitate a discussion on that topic.

7. Allow students the option to share what they wrote if their strip wasn't read out loud.

8. Repeat with the other emotions.

Reflection: What did you learn about your classmates' experiences?

Teacher Note: Read the strips silently before reading them to the class to ensure their appropriate.

Homework: Notice what other people are feeling.

LESSON 20: Feelings Exploration

Lesson Overview:

Activities in this Lesson:	About These Activities:
Opening Question	Asks students to share an experience about when their emotions changed.
Emotional Roller Coaster	Uses a classical theater game to practice identifying feelings.
Uncertain Feelings	Addresses numbness, feeling confused, and indifference.

SEL Standards: Self-Awareness / Relationship Skills

SEL Objectives: Identifying and Expressing Emotions

ACTIVITY 1: Opening Question

Time: 5 mins

Ask: "What caused your feelings to change?"

ACTIVITY 2: Emotional Roller Coaster

Time: 20 mins

Instructions:

1. Ask two students to volunteer to act out a scenario in front of the class.

2. Give the two students different characters to act out (the who), a conflict (the what), and a setting (the where).

3. Ask the class to suggest different emotions for each character to embody in their dialogue.

4. Freeze the dialogue at any moment and ask the class for new emotions for each character.

Sample Scenarios:

a. A customer complains to a store owner that the fruit they bought has mold and they want their money back. The store owner doesn't want to return the customer's money.

b. Two friends find a twenty-dollar bill on the sidewalk. One wants to keep it. The other wants to find the person who lost it.

c. One person on a beach wants to play their music loudly. Another person wants quiet.

Variation: Have the volunteers decide their own emotion and have the class guess what emotion they are expressing.

Reflections:
- How did the characters' emotions affect what was said?
- What is it like to experience a range of emotions?

ACTIVITY 3: Uncertain Feelings

Time: 20 mins

Instructions:
1. Ask, "Why are we sometimes unsure about what we are feeling?"

2. Say, "It might be that you have mixed feelings or you are feeling confused. Or if you are not feeling anything at all, you are feeling detached or numb."

3. Ask, "Why do you think that we sometimes don't feel anything?" (We get ridiculed for being sensitive, feelings hurt, they are held back).

4. Say, "The first step to take when you are not feeling anything, or feeling confused, is to just notice and name the disconnection. An optional second step is to become a feelings detective and try to figure out the feelings."

5. Divide the class into groups of 4–5 students.

6. Tell the groups to guess and discuss the feelings for each scenario.

   a. Your lunch is ordinary, you don't know where to sit and you don't have any desire to say anything.

   b. A friend of yours is mad at you and doesn't want to talk. You think you did not do anything wrong and they are mad for no reason.

   c. You like being with a friend but you think they are talking too much.

d. You notice your muscles are tight and you are staring at just one spot.

e. You are not thinking about anything.

f. You are playing a video game.

g. You notice your body is collapsing into the chair.

h. You just want the day to be done already.

i. Everything is just fine as it is.

j. Your friend is upset with you, wants to talk, and you have no idea why they are upset.

7. Have students share their results with the class.

Reflection: What have you learned about being a feelings detective?

Homework: Guess what someone is feeling.

LESSON 21: Feelings...Now What?

Lesson Overview:

Activities in this Lesson:	About These Activities:
Opening Question	Asks students to make a link between feelings and action.
Feelings and Action	Examines when feelings are a good guide to action and when they are not.
Triggers	Brings awareness to what positively and negatively influences how we feel.

SEL Standards: Self-Management

SEL Objectives: Impulse Control

ACTIVITY 1: Opening Question

Time: 5 mins

Ask: "When have you had a strong positive or negative feeling in your life? What action did you take?"

ACTIVITY 2: Feelings and Action

Time: 15–20 mins

Instructions:

1. Say, "Feelings help drive our actions and navigate the world around us."

   a. Feeling scared tells us to seek safety.

   b. Feeling disgusted makes it clear what we don't want.

   c. Happiness tells us what is great and worth doing again.

2. Ask, "What actions would you take after noticing these feelings in these situations?"

   a. Worried about a test the next day.

   b. Happy to share some time playing video games with a friend.

   c. Unsure about whether to hang out with some friends or go home.

   d. Mad that your friend is blaming you for something you didn't do.

   e. Bored eating the same breakfast every day.

3. Say, "Sometimes feelings aren't always the best guide to action. For example, you might hate a gift, but it can be socially awkward to tell someone that."

4. Ask, "When are feelings a good guide for action? When are they not?"

5. Divide the class into groups of 4–5 students.

6. Have each group share how they would feel in each scenario and what they consider to be the best course of action:

   a. Your friend wants to share their dessert with you.

   b. You lost a video game for the 8th time in a row.

   c. You get a perfect score on a quiz.

   d. You notice that some kids are screaming in the lunchroom.

   e. Your family forgets your birthday.

   f. You find a dollar on the floor in the hallway.

   g. You approve of a friend's fashion choice.

   h. Someone bumps into you from behind on the stairs.

   i. You are struggling with a math problem.

Reflection: When are feelings a good guide to action? When are they not?

ACTIVITY 3: Triggers

Time: 20–25 mins

Instructions:

1. Ask, "What triggers you?"

   Examples:

   a. Being blamed for something you didn't do,

   b. getting interrupted,

   c. someone being rude.

2. Say, "To control a trigger and not let a trigger control you, it's important to name the emotion, breathe, and evaluate the best course of action. These steps use the emotional part of the brain and the reasoning part of the brain."

3. Ask, "What can you do when you are triggered and you don't want to do something you will regret in the future?"

   Examples:

   a. Avoid the situation,

   b. Set a boundary with someone,

   c. Communicate what you feel.

4. Ask, "When in life do you get triggered positively?"

   Examples:

   a. Music pumps you up and triggers energy for a workout,

   b. An act of kindness triggers feelings of warmth,

   c. Connecting to nature calms you down.

5. How can you use positive triggers to get more of what you want in life?

6. Demonstrate making a poster by drawing a pathway that starts at the beginning of the day and ends at bedtime. Along the pathway, fill in events that are typical positive and negative triggers. Draw or write how you will respond or work with the triggers.

7. Give out paper to have students create their own trigger posters.

8. When students are finished, have students walk around the room to view each other's work.

Reflection: What did you notice about your relationship between feelings and actions?

Homework: Notice what decisions are driven by your feelings.

LESSON 22: Precision with Feelings, Thoughts, and Judgments

Lesson Overview:

Activities in this Lesson:	About These Activities:
Opening Question	Asks students to consider how feelings are different from thoughts.
Feelings and Thoughts	Helps students make an important distinction that will help them with self-connection.
Feelings with Hidden Judgments	Proclaims a separate category for feelings and offers new language for expression.
Feeling and Observation Practice	Gives students an opportunity to practice this new language.

SEL Standards: Self-Awareness / Relationship Skills

SEL Objectives: Identifying and Expressing Emotions / Self-Perception / Conflict Management

ACTIVITY 1: Opening Question

Time: 5 mins

Ask: "What's the difference between a feeling and a thought?"

ACTIVITY 2: Feelings and Thoughts

Time: 15–20 mins

Instructions:

1. Say, "Sometimes, people say they are feeling something, but they are actually expressing a thought."

   For Example:

   a. I feel you shouldn't have said that.

   b. I feel like going outside.

   c. I feel I am worse than everyone at this.

114

2. Say, "There is nothing wrong with these statements, but they are not expressing feelings. To be more precise, we can replace the word 'Feel' with 'Think.' It would have been more accurate to say:

    a. I think you shouldn't have said that.

    b. I think I want to go outside.

    c. I think I am worse than everyone at this."

3. Say, "Or you could express the feeling and the thought:

    a. I feel upset and you shouldn't have said that.

    b. I feel hyper and I want to go outside.

    c. I feel upset and I think I am worse than everyone at this."

4. Ask, "Which of these statements are feelings and which are thoughts? Why?"

    a. I feel that something is going to happen.

    b. I feel anxious about the test tomorrow.

    c. I am excited about the new version of 2K.

    d. I feel you are annoying.

    e. I am on my last nerve.

5. Ask, "How would you translate the statements that are thoughts into feelings?"

6. Ask, "Why might it be useful to be precise with the language of feelings?"

    Potential Answers:

    a. When you can name a feeling, you develop more self-connection.

    b. When you separate a feeling from a thought, it is easier for other people to empathize with your experience.

    c. Nobody can argue with a feeling. They can argue with a thought or judgment.

7. Say, "This is not an invitation to correct anyone else's mode of talking about feelings. Few people like to have their feelings corrected, even if the feelings may not actually be feelings."

Reflection: When will it be most useful for you to separate feelings from thoughts?

Teacher Note: This distinction may seem like a minor semantic adjustment, but the language distinction is crucial for future lessons in communication. Many conflicts start unconsciously by using judgmental language that is disconnected from feelings.

ACTIVITY 3: Feelings with Hidden Judgements

Time: 10–15 mins

Instructions:

1. Say, "When you state a feeling, you are expressing an experience that is only about you. There are some commonly used feeling words that aren't just about you, but are actually judging someone else. We are going to give these feelings a different name."

2. Ask, "What do you notice about these expressions of feelings?"

   a. I feel disrespected.

   b. I feel ignored.

   c. I feel criticized.

3. Say, "These feelings are expressing a judgment about what someone else is doing to them. These feelings can be renamed 'Feelings with Judgments.'"

4. Say, "These feelings are not wrong or bad, but they do contain judgements that can affect communication. Most people don't like to be judged. If you are able to communicate the feeling without judgment, you are expressing vulnerability and are more likely to be heard."

5. Say, "We are going to separate feelings that have judgments into feelings and observations. For example:

   a. The statement "I feel disrespected" can be translated to "I feel upset because you rolled your eyes at me."

116

b. The statement, "I feel ignored" can be translated to "I feel mad because you walked right by me and didn't say hi."

c. The statement, "I feel criticized" can be translated to "I feel confused because you said it was my fault.""

6. Divide the class into groups of 4–5 students.

7. Say, "Translate the following feelings with judgements into feelings and observations."

8. Write the following feelings in a place visible to everyone:

a. I feel betrayed.

b. I feel bullied.

c. I feel cheated.

d. I feel overworked.

e. I feel used.

Reflection: What is the value of expressing feelings with judgments in a different way?

ACTIVITY 4: Feelings and Observations Practice

Time: 10–15 mins

Instructions:
1. Divide students into groups of 4–5 students.

2. Ask each student to come up with a statement in response to each scenario. The statement must have a feeling and an observation.

   a. You notice a friend refused to share their dessert, but they have enough to share.

   b. Someone skips you in line.

   c. You answered a question from your teacher incorrectly.

   d. You forgot your best friend's birthday.

   e. You realize your homework doesn't make sense.

3. Have each group share their feelings statements.

Reflection: When would you use feelings and observations?

Homework:
- Notice the use of feelings that have hidden judgments.

- Try responding to a situation by expressing a feeling and observation.

UNIT 5: Empathy

▶ Translates judgments into compassion

▶ Builds community through empathy

▶ Introduces feeling, tonal, needs-based, and empathy similes

▶ Uses real-life experiences for practice and integration

LESSON 23: Feelings Empathy

Lesson Overview:

Activities in this Lesson:	About These Activities:
Opening Question	Introduces empathy through identifying someone's feelings.
Emotion Motion	Introduces empathy with a feelings guessing game.
What Empathy Isn't	Delves into the ways people respond to someone's feelings that are not empathetic.
Empathy Practice	Gives students the opportunity to practice empathy using real life feelings and experiences.

SEL Standards: Social Awareness / Relationship Skills

SEL Objectives: Empathy / Perspective-Taking / Communication

ACTIVITY 1: Opening Question

Time: 5 mins

Ask: "What do you do or say when you want to show you understand how someone feels?"

ACTIVITY 2: Emotion Motion

Time: 10–15 mins

Instructions:

1. Say, "Empathy means you understand someone else's emotion or experience. In this unit, we are going to explore a few different types of empathy."

2. Have Student A go outside the classroom. While that student is gone, the rest of the group chooses an emotion, such as joy or fear.

3. Have Student A return and choose an activity for the group to do together.

4. The group does the activity with their chosen emotion.

5. Student A then guesses the emotion.

6. Repeat with Student B leaving the room.

Variation: The class can choose the activity and the emotion. The student who leaves can guess both.

- What did you do to show emotion?
- What did you do to detect emotion?

ACTIVITY 3: What Empathy Isn't

Time: 10–15 mins

Instructions:

1. Say, "Now that we know what empathy is, we are going to define what empathy isn't."

2. Ask, "If you complain about losing a wallet and your friend tells you that they also lost their wallet, is this empathy?"

3. Say, "This is not wrong or bad, but it's not empathy. This response is called, 'Me too.'"

4. Ask, "If you get a bad grade on a test and someone responds by giving advice on how to study next time, is this empathy?"

5. Say, "This response is advice and can be helpful, but it's not empathy."

6. Ask, "If someone's girlfriend breaks up with them, and you ask them what they did wrong, is this empathy?"

7. Say, "This is interrogation and not empathy."

8. Ask, "If a friend shares their disappointment over their dry turkey sandwich and you tell them they should be happy they are not going to starve, is this empathy?"

9. Say, "This is dismissive. This is not empathy."

10. Say, "Now that we know what empathy is and isn't, let's practice empathy."

Reflection: How does empathy differ from other responses?

122

ACTIVITY 4: Empathy Practice

Time: 10–15 mins

Supplies: A feelings list for each student

A full size version of this worksheet is available in the appendix.

☺ Feelings Associated with Met Needs ☺

Excited	**Happy**	**Hopeful**
Energetic	Blissful	Confident
Enthusiastic	Delighted	Expectant
Passionate	Joyful	Light hearted
Surprised	Pleased	Upbeat
Inspired	**Interested**	**Peaceful**
Amazed	Curious	Refreshed
Motivated	Enchanted	Relaxed
Psyched	Fascinated	Relieved
Stirred	Intrigued	Satisfied

☹ Feelings Associated with Unmet Needs ☹

Anger	**Bored**	**Confused**
Aggravated	Apathetic	Dazed
Annoyed	Disconnected	Mixed
Enraged	Distant	Mystified
Frustrated	Numb	Torn
Disgust	**Fatigue**	**Fear**
Bothered	Burnt out	Nervous
Dislike	Sleepy	Panicked
Horrified	Tired	Scared
Repulsed	Weary	Worried
Pain	**Sadness**	**Uneasy**
Aching	Depressed	Disturbed
Agony	Disappointed	Embarrassed
Hurting	Hopeless	Uncomfortable
Lonely	Miserable	Upset

*This list is modified from a Feelings List by NYCNVC.

123

Instructions:

1. Demonstrate giving a student empathy by listening to them and then using the feelings list to guess what they might be feeling.

2. Say, "An empathy guess is given with curiosity and formatted as a question. You are a partner in trying to help the speaker figure out what they might be feeling without any other additional comments."

3. Divide students into pairs and give each student a feelings list.

4. Ask Student A to share anything that is on their mind for one minute.

5. Ask Student B to listen silently. At the end of one minute, ask Student B to guess what Student A is feeling.

6. Switch roles.

7. Repeat the empathy process, but in round two, the listener can give an empathy guess at any time.

Reflection: How did it feel to receive empathy?

Homework: Guess what people are feeling without saying anything.

LESSON 24: Connection through Tone

Lesson Overview:

Activities in this Lesson:	About These Activities:
Opening Question	Asks students to think about tone.
Tonal Empathy	Is an advanced form of empathy that integrates awareness of the tone of one's voice.
Tonal Empathy Practice	Uses the game Jenga to create intense moments that could be assisted by tonal empathy.

SEL Standards: Social Awareness/Relationship Skills

SEL Objectives: Empathy/Social Engagement

ACTIVITY 1: Opening Question

Time: 5 mins

Ask: "What tone do you use when you want people to take you seriously?"

ACTIVITY 2: Tonal Empathy

Time: 10 mins

Instructions:
1. Have students stand and form a circle.
2. Have Student A say how they are feeling using an expressive tone.
3. Have the class repeat Student A's feeling with the same tone of voice.
4. Moving clockwise in the circle, have each student share how they are feeling using an expressive tone and then have the class repeat the feeling with the same tone of voice.

Reflection: How does tone affect empathy?

ACTIVITY 3: Tonal Empathy Practice

Time: 30 mins

Supplies: 6 boxes of Jenga

Instructions:
1. Divide the class into groups of four.
2. Give each group a game.
3. Stop every five minutes to do an empathy guess. Student A shares first and Student B gives an empathetic guess. Then switch roles.

Reflection: What did it feel like when someone connected to not only your feelings, but your tone of voice?

Homework: Notice what tone people use to express their feelings.

LESSON 25: Values Empathy

Lesson Overview:

Activities in this Lesson:	About These Activities:
Opening Question	Introduces universal needs.
All About Needs	Explores and assesses universal needs in our lives.
Needs Charades	Is a theatrical game offering a fun way to guess someone's needs.
Needs Empathy Practice	Gives students the opportunity to practice needs empathy using real life feelings and experiences.

SEL Standards: Social Awareness, Relationship Skills

SEL Objectives: Empathy / Perspective-Taking / Social Engagement

ACTIVITY 1: Opening Questions

Time: 5–10 mins

Ask:
1. "What does everyone need for survival?"
2. "Besides physical needs, what does everyone need to survive?"

ACTIVITY 2: All About Needs

Time: 15–20 mins

Instructions:

1. Say, "Another type of empathy is called 'Needs Empathy.' We connect to other people by considering what they might be needing in their lives. With Needs empathy, we consider needs that are not specific to one person, but universal to everyone."

2. Ask, "What are universal needs? What does everyone in the world need?" Write responses on a chart or marker board.

3. Usually students start with physical needs (water, food, shelter, sleep, etc,) and then share other universal needs (love, belonging, respect, etc.).

4. Explain that universal needs are distinct from individual needs. "I need my friend to give me my money back" is not a universal need because not everyone in the world needs to get money back from your friend. Universal needs are not specific to a particular person, action, or object.

5. Say, "If you need someone to do something, it is not a universal need because not everyone in the world needs that person to do that thing. Universal needs are only what everyone experiences. A specific need is a strategy to achieve a universal need."

6. Ask, "Which are universal needs and which are strategies to achieve a universal need?"

    a. I need you to stop bothering me.

    b. I need understanding.

    c. I need sleep.

    d. I need my friend to give me my money back.

7. Say, "We are going to look at a Needs list. On the left side of each Need, on a scale of 1–10, rate how important that need is to you."

8. Say, "On the right side of every Need, write down how much do you have this Need in your life on a scale of 1–10."

A full size version of this worksheet is available in the appendix.

AUTONOMY	CONNECTION (cont.)	PEACE
Choice	Self-connection	Acceptance
Dignity	Self-expression	Balance
Freedom	Shared Reality	Beauty
Independence	Stability	Ease
Self-expression	Support	Faith
Space	To know and be known	Harmony
Spontaneity	To see and be seen	Hope
	Trust	Order
CONNECTION	Understanding	Peace-of-mind
Acceptance	Warmth	Space
Affection		
Appreciation	**MEANING**	**PHYSICAL WELL-BEING**
Authenticity	Awareness	Air
Belonging	Celebration	Care
Care	Challenge	Comfort
Closeness	Clarity	Food
Communication	Competence	Movement/Exercise
Communion	Consciousness	Rest/Sleep
Community	Contribution	Safety
Companionship	Creativity	Self-care
Compassion	Discovery	Shelter
Consideration	Efficiency	Water
Empathy	Effectiveness	
Friendship	Growth	**PLAY**
Inclusion	Integration	Adventure
Inspiration	Integrity	Excitement
Integrity	Learning	Fun
Intimacy	Mourning	Humor
Love	Movement	Joy
Mutuality	Participation	Relaxation
Nurturing	Perspective	
Partnership	Presence	
Presence	Progress	
Respect/Self-respect	Purpose	
Security	Self-expression	
Self-acceptance	Understanding	
Self-care		

* This list is modified from a Needs List by NYCNVC

9. Ask, "How do you feel after connecting to your needs?"

10. Say, "When you identify your needs, you learn your motivation behind everything you do think or feel. Then you can understand others in a more compassionate way. It can be a road map towards connection, satisfaction and happiness."

Reflection: Which need did you resonate with the most?

Teacher Note: Universal needs are part of an approach to empathy developed by Marshall Rosenberg called Nonviolent Communication. It takes extensive training to teach Nonviolent Communication. Go to Nycnvc.org for training opportunities. This lesson is only a brief introduction. However, even a brief exposure to universal needs can be profound.

ACTIVITY 3: Needs Charades

Time: 10–15 mins

Instructions: 1. Divide the class into groups of 5–8 students.

2. Ask for one student to talk about a life situation with a specific need in mind.

   Example:

   a. If a student has a need for consideration, they might say, "Everyone in my family is talking about where we might go on vacation, but no one has asked me."

   b. If a student has a need for choice, they might say, "Everyday I have to do my homework as soon as I get home."

3. It's the task of the other students to guess the need.

Reflection: How did you figure out the need that someone was expressing?

ACTIVITY 4: Needs Empathy Practice

Time: 5–10 mins

Instructions:
1. Divide the class into pairs.

2. Have Student A share something that happened to them that day.

3. Using the Needs list, Student B then asks, "Are you needing…?" and guesses the need.

4. Student A thanks Student B for the guess and considers whether that need resonates with them.

5. Switch roles.

Reflections:
- What was it like to receive needs empathy?

- How did needs empathy compare to feelings empathy?

Homework: Analyze in any given moment what someone else is needing.

LESSON 26: All Roads Lead to Needs

Lesson Overview:

Activities in this Lesson:	About These Activities:
Opening Question	Links what students feel to what they need.
Met and Unmet Needs	Looks at feeling fulfilled and unfulfilled.
Judgments and Needs	Offers a method for translating our judgements into compassionate understanding.
More Needs Empathy Practice	Gives students more training to perceive people's needs.

SEL Standards: Social Awareness / Relationship Skills

SEL Objectives: Empathy / Relationship Building

ACTIVITY 1: Opening Question

Time: 5 mins

Ask: "What are you feeling and what do you need?"

ACTIVITY 2: Met and Unmet Needs

Time: 15–20 mins

Supplies: A class set of feelings and needs sheets

Instructions:

1. Say, "It can be useful to notice our met needs in addition to our unmet needs."

2. Hand out a feelings / needs list for each student.

3. Ask, "What needs are met for you right now?"

4. Ask, "How do you feel after noticing your met needs?"

5. Say, "When our needs are met, we are likely to be experiencing positive feelings. When needs are not met, we are likely to be experiencing negative feelings. Feelings are a great communicator of our met and unmet needs."

6. Say, "If someone is feeling positive, you can guess, 'Are you feeling happy with a met need of appreciation?'"

7. "If someone is feeling negative, you can guess, 'Are you feeling disappointed with a need for respect?'"

8. Ask for a volunteer to go outside the classroom.

9. While Student A is gone, the rest of the group chooses an emotion and a met or unmet need.

   Example:

   a. Feeling disappointed with an unmet need for respect.

   b. Feeling joy with an met need for friendship.

   c. Feeling confused with an unmet need for clarity.

10. Have Student A return to the classroom the rest of the class acts out the feeling and talks about the need without giving it away.

11. Give Student A three guesses.

12. Repeat with Student B leaving the room.

Reflection:

• Do you find it useful to identify your met needs?

• What did you notice about the relationship between feelings and needs?

ACTIVITY 3: Judgments and Needs

Time: 15–20 mins

Instructions:

1. Ask, "A lot of people say 'Don't judge!' because judging people alienates people, but is it possible to not judge?"

2. Say, "While it may not be possible to stop judging, translating your judgements into needs is definitely possible. The theory about Needs is that everything you do, think, and feel is an attempt to meet a need. Judgments are no different."

3. Ask, "If you are judging someone for being rude, what need might be behind that judgment?" Discuss.

4. Ask, "If you are judging someone's fashion choice, what need might be behind that judgment?" Discuss.

5. Ask, "If you are judging someone for missing a jump shot, what need might be behind that judgment?" Discuss.

6. Divide the class into groups of four or five.

7. Ask the group to translate these judgments into Needs:

   a. It's always so quiet here.

   b. Those colors don't match.

   c. That answer was stupid.

   d. They look good together.

   e. She talks too much.

   f. He is always helping people.

8. Ask the group to then translate the judgments into what the other person needs.

Reflection: What is the benefit of translating judgments into needs?

ACTIVITY 4: Needs Empathy Practice

Time: 5–10 mins

Instructions:
1. Divide the class into pairs.

2. Say, "We are going to practice Needs Empathy again. This time, you can ask someone if they have a met or unmet need for _____ and give a needs empathy guess."

3. Have Student A share something that happened to them that day or anything they are thinking about.

4. Using the Needs list, Student B gives an empathy guess.

5. Student A thanks Student B for the guess and considers whether that need resonates with them.

6. Switch roles.

Reflection: How does knowing people are trying to have their needs met change your perception of the world?

Homework: Translate someone's judgments into a guess about their needs.

LESSON 27: Empathy Similes

Lesson Overview:

Activities in this Lesson:	About These Activities:
Opening Question	Considers the importance of metaphors.
Simile Check In	Uses postcards to describe what we are feeling.
Empathy Simile	Is a creative form of empathy.
Toothpick on a Bottle	Is an opportunity to practice simile empathy while attempting a challenging task.

SEL Standards: Social Awareness / Relationship Skills

SEL Objectives: Empathy, Social Engagement

ACTIVITY 1: Opening Question

Time: 5 mins

Ask: "What are your favorite similes?

ACTIVITY 2: Simile Check In

Time: 5–10 min

Supplies: 40 Postcards

Set up: Place the postcards in the middle of the floor with the pictures face up.

Instructions:
1. Say, "Choose one postcard that best represents how you feel right now."
2. After everyone has chosen a card, go around the room and have each student share the card they chose with an option to share why they chose it.

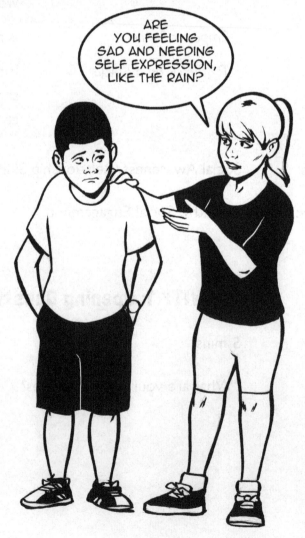

ACTIVITY 3: Empathy Simile

Time: 15–20 mins

Instructions:

1. Have students meet in groups of four.

2. Student A shares what they are feeling.

3. The other three students then compete to create the best simile that demonstrates empathy.

4. Have Student A thank everyone for their contribution, but select one simile as their favorite.

5. Change roles so that everyone gets a chance to share their feelings and judge other students' similes.

   Sample Similes:

   a. Are you feeling sad and needing self expression like the rain? (weather)

   b. Are you feeling upbeat and have a met need for excitement like electricity? (science)

   c. Are you feeling up and down and needing resilience like basketball? (sports)

   d. Are you feeling clear and having a met need of transparency like the window? (anything in the room)

ACTIVITY 4: Toothpick on Bottle Pass

Time: 15–20 mins

Supplies: Box of toothpicks and one water bottle for each group

Instructions:

1. Divide the class into groups of 4–6 students.

2. Give each student three toothpicks and each group one water bottle.

3. Tell the class the task is for each student to lay one toothpick across the top of the bottle opening and pass it to the next student in the group.

4. If a toothpick drops at any point, all the toothpicks are returned and the challenge starts from the beginning.

5. After each pass, have one person at a time get empathy with a simile from the other students.

6. Round Two: take the toothpicks off the bottle one at a time.

7. Round Three: stack the toothpicks two at a time.

8. Round Four: pass the bottle with the non-dominant hand.

Reflection: Was empathy with similes more or less effective for you?

Homework: Show someone empathy by using a simile.

UNIT 6: Communication

▶ Teaches tools for effective communication

▶ Reveals methods for conflict resolution

▶ Explores communication styles

▶ Analyzes how intention affects conversations

LESSON 28: Effective and Ineffective Communication

Lesson Overview:

Activities in this Lesson:	About These Activities:
Opening Question	Asks students to reflect on what effective communication is.
Quick Look	Reveals the challenge of effective communication.
Shared Definition	Asks students to create a communal definition of communication.
Lost at Sea	Is a dialogue exercise in which students will have to make tough choices.

SEL Standards: Relationship Skills

SEL Objectives: Communication

ACTIVITY 1: Opening Question

Time: 5 mins

Ask: "When have you successfully or unsuccessfully communicated?"

ACTIVITY 2: Quick Look

Time: 20–25 mins

Supplies: 6 sets of Lego pieces

Instructions:

1. Create a Lego structure with one set of Lego pieces and hide it in a part of the room where no one can see it.

2. Divide the class into 5 equally sized groups and give them each a set of the same Lego pieces.

3. Explain that in the first round, one member from the group will be able to view the model structure for ten seconds. They will then have one minute to instruct the rest of the group on how to build it.

4. The viewer from each group can not physically help construct the Lego structure. When the minute is over, they must watch the rest of the activity in silence.

5. When the first round is complete, a new member of the group will repeat the same process.

6. Repeat until only one student remains building the structure.

7. Bring out the original structure and compare the results.

8. Repeat, but this time, allowing communication after one minute.

Reflection: What did you learn about effective communication?

ACTIVITY 3: Shared Definition

Time: 5–10 mins

Instructions:

1. Say, "The second task is to come up with a shared definition of communication, what is necessary for effective communication, and what makes communication difficult at times."

2. After groups are finished, have every group share.

Reflection: How have your definition and understanding of communication changed after this activity?

ACTIVITY 4: Lost at Sea

Time: 10–15 mins

Instructions:

1. Tell each group to imagine they are lost at sea on a raft.

2. The group can choose 8 of the following 12 items:

   a. 5 gallons of water

   b. a mirror

   c. a bucket

   d. a rope

   e. a waterproof tarp

   f. a blanket

g. a first-aid kit

h. a fishing rod

i. a knife

j. 20 canned meals

k. a radio

l. a compass

3. Have the group debate which items they would choose to have on their raft.

4. After 5–10 minutes, have each group share the eight items they chose and why.

Reflection: Did you experience effective or ineffective communication today?

Homework: Notice examples of effective and ineffective communication in your life.

LESSON 29: Paraphrase Request

Lesson Overview:

Activities in this Lesson:	About These Activities:
Opening Question	Asks how to achieve more certainty in communication.
Communication Breakdown with Paraphrase Request	Is a slight variation of the game Communication Breakdown, but this time, students will ask other students to paraphrase what they heard them say.
Dialogue with Paraphrase Request	Uses engaging conversation topics to practice effective communication through paraphrase requests.

SEL Standards: Relationship Skills / Social Awareness

SEL Objectives: Communication / Perspective-Taking

ACTIVITY 1: Opening Question

Time: 5 mins

Ask: "How can you make sure someone else understands what you said?"

ACTIVITY 2: Communication Breakdown with Paraphrase Request

Time: 15–20 mins

Instructions: 1. Ask for 5 students to leave the room.

2. Choose Student A to tell a quick three or four sentence story.

3. Ask one student, Student B, to return from outside the room.

4. Have Student A share their story with Student B.

5. Student B asks for Student C to come in from outside the classroom.

6. In front of class, Student B relates Student A's story to Student C.

7. Student C asks for Student D to come in from outside of the classroom.

8. Student C then shares what he or she heard to student B.

9. Repeat until the story is shared five times.

10. Round Two: play again, but allow the speaker to ask the listener, "What did you hear me say?" and make any necessary corrections if they heard incorrectly.

11. Ask, "What is the difference between requesting someone share what they heard you say and demanding they do it?"

12. Ask, "How can you phrase the question so you don't seem demanding?"

Reflection: How much more clarity was gained once you requested other students to paraphrase what they heard them say?

ACTIVITY 3: Dialogue with Paraphrase Request

Time: 15–20 mins

Instructions:
1. Ask, "What is the best action film of all time?"

2. Call on Student A. When Student A has finished giving an answer, have them call on Student B.

3. Tell Student A to ask Student B what Student B heard Student A said before Student B shares their own answer.

4. Student B shares what they heard Student A first before sharing their own answer.

5. Choose other genres as time permits.

Reflection: What is the value in asking someone what they heard you say?

Homework: Ask one person, but not an adult, to share what they heard you say as politely as possible.

LESSON 30: Communication Styles

Lesson Overview:

Activities in this Lesson:	About These Activities:
Opening Question	Asks students to consider their communication style.
Communication Style Assessment	Examines passive, assertive, and aggressive communication responses.
Resting Rulers	Challenges students to be mindful of their communication style.

SEL Standards: Self-Awareness / Relationship Skills

SEL Objectives: Self-Perception / Communication

ACTIVITY 1: Opening Question

Time: 5 mins

Ask: "Do you consider yourself a passive, assertive, or aggressive person? Why?"

ACTIVITY 2: Communication Style Assessment

Time:

15–20 mins

Instructions:

1. Ask, "What are the positives and negatives of communicating passively, assertively, and aggressively?"

2. Ask, "In what situations is it best to be passive, assertive, and aggressive?"

3. Ask, "How can we moderate aggressive behavior when it is more useful to be assertive?" (Students will usually answer by addressing speaking volume, using personal attacks, and body language.)

4. Ask, "How can we be more assertive when we are being too passive?"

5. Ask, "When can being passive be aggressive?" (A good example of this is when students don't do anything during group work and then aggressively judge the results.)

6. Ask the class which communication style they would use in each situation and what they would say.

   a. Your family forgot your birthday?

   b. Someone accused you of stealing their dessert, but you didn't.

   c. During a group project, no one else will do work but you.

   d. Someone insults the clothes you are wearing.

   e. Someone accidently spilled a cup of water on you?

Reflection: What did you learn about each communication style?

ACTIVITY 3: Resting Rulers

Time: 15–20 mins

Supplies: 6 rulers

Instructions:
1. Divide the class into groups of 4–5 students.

2. Give each group a ruler.

3. Ask each student to place an index finger under the ruler.

4. Tell the class their task is to collectively take the ruler from a horizontal position to a vertical position and then rest it on the ground.

5. Students can not use any of their other fingers, nor can they remove their finger from under the ruler.

6. Assure students there is a solution to this challenge.

7. If necessary, offer a hint that they can use an object.

8. Ask students, "What communication style did you use in this activity?"

Reflection: What is your dominant communication style?

Homework: Notice the communication styles of different people.

LESSON 31: Communication Tools

Lesson Overview:

Activities in this Lesson:	About These Activities:
Opening Question	Asks students to share when they have witnessed arguments that have escalated in intensity and consider why the argument intensified.
Observation and Judgment	Introduces a communication skill used in conflict resolution.
Observation and Requests Practice	Gives students real world scenarios to practice the skill of sharing observations and making requests.
Requests and Demands	Offers the possibility for dialogue and participation instead of demanding someone to do something.

SEL Standards: Relationship Skills

SEL Objectives: Communication

ACTIVITY 1: Opening Question

Time: 5 mins

Ask: "When have you had an argument that escalated or became more heated? What happened?"

ACTIVITY 2: Observation and Judgment

Time: 15–20 mins

Instructions:
1. Ask, "Why do some verbal conflicts get solved and others worsen?"

2. Say, "The way we speak can escalate or de-escalate conflict. When we use language that blames, insults, or criticizes someone, the conflict can get worse."

3. Ask, "How do you react when someone blames you for something, insults you, labels you, or criticizes you?"

4. Ask, "If these tactics don't work, why do we communicate this way?" (We don't know a different way to handle conflict.)

5. Say, "Observational language allows you to express yourself without escalating conflict."

6. Ask, "How do statements A and B differ?"

   a. Statement A, "You are nosy."

   b. Statement B, "You ask a lot of questions about my life."

7. Say, "Observational language doesn't communicate judgment. Observational language only communicates facts."

8. Ask, "Is this statement an observation or a judgment?"

   a. My teacher was picking on me for no reason.

   b. Twenty people liked my post.

   c. Nobody asked for my opinion.

157

d. She burped.

e. Your handwriting is sloppy.

9. Divide the class into groups of 4–5 students.

10. Tell each group to translate the judgements into observational language:

    a. You shouldn't be talking about other people.

    b. Green and purple don't go together.

    c. You disrespected me.

    d. This class is boring.

    e. People play too much.

Reflection: How does using observational language assist clear communication?

Teacher Note: It can be useful to do a lesson on language that triggers students and translating that language into observations. Trigger language can include insults, catastrophizing, and stating one's opinion as a fact.

ACTIVITY 3: Requests and Demands

Time: 10–15 mins

Instructions:

1. Ask, "When someone demands you do something, how do you respond?"

2. Ask, "When someone requests you do something, how do you respond?"

3. Ask, "What's the benefit of a demand and what's the benefit of a request?"

4. Ask, "What's the disadvantage of a command? What's the disadvantage of a request?"

5. Say, "The most effective requests are:

a. Framed positively so you state what you want, not what you don't want.

b. Specific and doable.

c. Not demanding someone to say yes."

6. Say, "Let's convert these statements from demands into requests."

a. Give me that book.

b. Pass the ball.

c. Don't bump into me.

d. Don't tell anyone.

7. Say, "Let's improve these requests."

a. Can you stop bothering me?

b. Can you not be selfish?

c. Will you text me?

d. Will you listen for once?

8. Say, "If someone says no to your request, ask them why they said no or consider a different request in which they might say yes. If you do not allow someone to say, "No," then you are not making a request. You are making a demand."

Reflection: When is it appropriate to use a request and when is it appropriate to use a demand?

ACTIVITY 4: Observation and Request Practice

Time: 5–10 mins

Instructions:

1. Say, "We are now going to combine both communication tools to handle conflicts."

2. Ask, "How can you respond using an observation and a request to these situations?"

   a. Your best friend is hanging out with other people who annoy you.

   b. Someone you were playing video games with seems to be using cheat codes to beat you.

   c. Your friends are misbehaving because there's a substitute teacher.

   d. A friend of yours spoils a movie for you.

Reflection: How did using observations and requests influence communication?

Homework: Use observational language and requests when you have a conflict.

LESSON 32: "I" Statement

Lesson Overview:

Activities in this Lesson:	About These Activities:
Opening Question	Asks how to be assertive.
I Statement Practice	Teaches a transformational communication tool.
I Statement Role Play	Asks the class to assist two students having a conflict by using "I" statements.

SEL Standards: Relationship Skills

SEL Objectives: Communication

ACTIVITY 1: Opening Question

Time: 5 mins

Ask: "When you are upset, how can you express yourself assertively without being either passive or aggressive?"

ACTIVITY 2: "I" Statement Practice

Time: 20–25 mins

Instructions:

1. Say, "Nobody likes to be accused, insulted, or blamed, and yet this is how people often communicate when something goes wrong."

2. Ask, "Why do people communicate like this during conflicts?" (It seems like an effective way to express oneself.)

3. Say, "There is a tool for communicating your thinking that is more effective, doesn't escalate conflict, and increases the chances of being heard. It's called an "I" statement."

4. Share the four parts of an "I" statement:

   a. Part 1: Say how you feel.

   b. Part 2: Share the behavior that triggered the feeling.

   c. Part 3: Explain the reason why this behavior affected you.

   d. Part 4: Ask for what you want.

5. Share the formula, I feel _____ when you _____ because _____. Can you _____?

6. Give three examples of an "I" statement:

   a. I am upset when you leave without saying goodbye because I am worried you don't care. Can you say goodbye before leaving?

   b. I am mad when you don't pass the ball because we are a team. Can you pass the ball more?

   c. I am disappointed that you didn't pay me back because you said you would have the money today. Can you pay me tomorrow?

7. Ask, "What do you notice about the "I" statements?"

8. Ask, "Why are "I" statements effective?"

9. Divide the class into groups of four or five students.

I FEEL _____ WHEN YOU _____ BECAUSE _____ . CAN YOU _____ ?

10. Say, "Convert these statements into "I" statements:

   a. You move too fast.

   b. You messed up.

   c. Why don't you ever listen?

   d. Why are you always late?

   e. You didn't text me when you said you would.

   f. You left this place a mess.

11. After 5 minutes, have each group share their answers.

Reflection: What are the advantages and disadvantages of using an "I" statement?

ACTIVITY 3: "I" Statement Role Play

Time: 10–15 mins

Instructions: 1. Ask for two volunteers to act out a scenario.

2. Ask the class for a common conflict between two people the students will role play.

3. First, have Student A and Student B try to solve the conflict without "I" statements.

4. After a minute or two, have Student A and Student B try to solve the same conflict using "I" statements.

5. Allow the class to interject by raising their hands and offering suggestions for I statements.

6. Say, "I" statements don't solve or end conflict, but they are an effective tool for not escalating conflict, being heard, and taking responsibility for your feelings and communicating your experience."

Reflection: Do you prefer Observation and Requests or "I" statements?

Homework: Try to use an I statement when something bothers you.

LESSON 33: Intention

Lesson Overview:

Activities in this Lesson:	About These Activities:
Opening Question	Considers intention in a conversation.
Being Right	Examines the effects of making oneself right and someone else wrong in communication.
Truth and Communication	Challenges the habit of thinking we have sole knowledge over what is true.
Intention Practice	Uses a role play exercise to practice observing one's mindset in a conversation.

SEL Standards: Self-Awareness / Relationship Skills

SEL Objectives: Self-Perception / Communication

ACTIVITY 1: Opening Question

Time: 5 mins

Ask: "How do you react when someone wants to prove you wrong?"

ACTIVITY 2: Being Right

Time: 15–20 mins

Instructions:

1. Say, "Sometimes, it's not what you say, but the way you say it. If you notice your intentions in communication, it will influence your words, your tone, and your results."

2. Ask, "When one person is pushing to be right or make you wrong, how does that influence their words, tone, and results?"

3. Ask, "Why do we like to be right? Why is it hard to not have this intention?" (We have been communicating in this way for a long time. Righteous communication feels powerful and effective. We think we can force our perspective onto someone else.)

4. Say, "We are usually good at detecting when someone else just wants to be right, but not as good at seeing when we are just trying to be right ourselves."

5. Ask, "How can you tell whether you are just trying to be right when you are communicating?"

6. Say, "Here are some questions to ask yourself in order to clarify your intention in a conversation:

   Before the conversation:

   a. Why am I having this conversation? What is my goal?

   b. Am I curious about someone else's perspective?

   c. Am I seeking to satisfy what I want or am I thinking about what's best for everyone?

   During the conversation:

   a. What is my tone of voice? What does my body language say?

   b. Am I evaluating the validity of their logic or just trying to prove them wrong?

   c. Am I using blaming language?

   d. Am I just trying to get my way or am I thinking about everyone's needs?"

7. Say, "Think of a conflict that you have with someone. Think about why you are right, why they are wrong, and what you want to do about it."

8. Say, "Use the 'Before the conversation' questions and notice your intention."

9. Ask, "How do you think the conversation will go?"

10. Say, "Now think about that same conflict. Think about the conflict from their perspective."

11. Ask, "What are their needs? What questions would you ask them to try to understand their experience?"

12. Ask, "How do you think the conversation will go?"

13. Ask, "If you notice you are communicating with only the intention to be right, what can you do to change your approach to a conversation?"

Reflection: How does intention affect conversation?

ACTIVITY 3: Truth and Communication

Time: 10–15 mins

Instructions:

1. Mark a blank paper with a blue X on one side and a red X on the other side.

2. Show the class the blue X without letting them see the red X on the other side.

3. Ask, "What color is the X on the paper?"

4. Explain, "The color of the X is red."

5. Facilitate a discussion about the color.

6. If appropriate, give a clue by saying, "Another color of the X is red."

7. After a few minutes, show both sides.

8. Ask, "What does this activity teach us about truth and communicating effectively?"

Reflection: What do you know to be true that may only be an incomplete depiction of a greater truth?

ACTIVITY 4: Intention Practice

Time: 10–15 mins

Instructions:
1. Divide students into pairs.

2. Say, "We are going to practice noticing our intention in a role play. Student A will play the role of a student who feels they are being unfairly picked on by a teacher. Student B will play the role of the teacher.

   a. In the first round, Student A will approach the scenario with a right / wrong intention.

   b. In the second round, Student A will approach the scenario with a more collaborative intention.

Reflection: What did you learn about intention and results?

Homework: Notice your intention in your conversations.

UNIT 7: Integrity

▶ Examines right, wrong, and the effectiveness of rules

▶ Explores the value of keeping your word

▶ Seeks creative solutions instead of excuses

▶ Evaluates the importance of integrity within a group

LESSON 34: Morality

Lesson Overview:

Activities in this Lesson:	About These Activities:
Opening Question	Asks students about when they had to decide between right and wrong.
Right and Wrong	Explores the concept of morality.
Honesty	Examines the complexity of being completely honest.
What Would You Do?	Explores the role of integrity in decision-making.

SEL Standards: Responsible Decision-Making

SEL Objectives: Evaluating / Reflecting / Ethical Responsibility

ACTIVITY 1: Opening Question

Time: 5 mins

Ask: "When in your life did you have to make a tough decision between right and wrong? What did you choose? Why?"

ACTIVITY 2: Right and Wrong

Time: 15–20 mins

Instructions:
1. Say, "We are going to study integrity in this unit. The dictionary defines integrity as, "Adherence to a moral code." This is an advanced way of saying, 'Doing what is right.'

2. Ask, "Why do we sometimes struggle between what we know is right and wrong?" (We feel we can get away with it. We emphasize what is good for us instead of the group. We don't agree with societal expectations. We want to be happy now and are not thinking of long term consequences).

Add Optional Questions:

a. Do you do the right thing when no one is watching? Why or why not?

b. Why do you think others struggle between doing what's right and wrong?

c. What is the benefit to us and the world when we do what's right?

d. What is the harm when we do what's wrong?

e. How do you feel when you do the right thing?

f. How do you feel when you do the wrong thing?

g. Is morality universal? What morals are universal? Which ones are not?

h. Where does morality come from? What are the benefits of morality?

Reflections:

• How does reflecting about morality affect you?

• What are the advantages and disadvantages of thinking about what is right and wrong?

ACTIVITY 3: Honesty

Time: 10–15 mins

Instructions:

1. Say, "Honesty is an important part of integrity."

2. Ask,

   a. "Why is honesty important?"

   b. "Why are people sometimes dishonest?"

   c. "Why is it difficult to be honest when you make a mistake?"

   d. "Is it always best to say what you think and be honest?"

e. "How can you share honestly without hurting someone's feelings?"

f. "What's the best way to handle someone who is being dishonest?"

Reflection: What is your relationship with honesty?

ACTIVITY 4: What Would You Do?

Time: 10–15 mins

Instructions:
1. Divide the class into groups of four or five students.

2. Decide as a group what the right thing to do is in each scenario:

   a. If you agreed to sell something to a friend and you said you would bring it to school the next day, but someone later offered you more money for it, what would you do and why?

   b. A friend offers you the answers to a test before you take it. What do you do?

   c. You do something wrong, but someone else gets in trouble for it. They get suspended. Do you admit the truth?

   d. You are attracted to your friend's ex. What do you do?

3. Ask students to share their own scenarios.

Reflection: What did you find interesting about the discussion about right and wrong?

Homework: Notice whether people act with integrity or not.

LESSON 35: Rules

Lesson Overview:

Activities in this Lesson:	About These Activities:
Opening Question	Asks about the role of rules in our life.
Rules Discussion	Reflects upon the importance of rules.
With and Without Rules	Illuminates the value of rules using an experiential exercise.
Pulse	Is a fun, competitive game that is successful only when students follow the rules.

SEL Standards: Responsible Decision-Making / Relationship Skills

SEL Objectives: Ethical Responsibility / Teamwork

ACTIVITY 1: Opening Question

Time: 5 mins

Ask: "What are some good and bad rules in school, at home, and in the world?"

ACTIVITY 2: Rules Discussion

Time: 5–10 mins

Instructions: 1. Pose questions to the class:

   a. What is the importance of rules?

   b. What happens when people break the rules?

   c. What rules do people break that upset? Why do you think they break them?

   d. What is the best way to handle unjust rules?

Reflection: What is your relationship with rules?

ACTIVITY 3: With And Without Rules

Time: 10–15 mins

Instructions:

2. Have students play Rock, Paper, Scissors, but allow students to change rules as they please, without harming each other and the environment.

3. After 3 minutes, have students play again with rules.

4. Discuss the difference.

Reflection: What happens when rules are broken?

ACTIVITY 4: Pulse

Time: 20–25 mins

Instructions:

1. Have students sit in a circle and divide the class into two teams.

2. Leave an empty chair on one end of the circle and sit on the opposite end, evenly dividing the group.

3. If there is an odd number of students, ask one student to be a judge.

4. Place an object on the empty chair—anything that isn't fragile. A stuffed animal is ideal.

5. Announce that you will be flipping a coin.

6. Only the two students sitting next to the teacher can have their eyes open. These students are the coin readers and will pass the result of the coin flip to their teammates.

7. Everyone else has their eyes closed and there is no talking.

8. If the result of the coin flip is heads, the coin reader will tap the thigh of the person next to them and then that person taps their neighbor's thigh. These taps continue until the last person on the team is tapped.

9. When the last person on the team next to the empty chair is tapped, they can grab the object on the empty chair.

10. The first team to grab the object gets a point for their team.

11. If the result of the coin flip is tails, the coin reader will do nothing.

12. Students can not tap their neighbor until they are tapped, even if they hear someone else being tapped.

13. If the Coin Reader sees tails, but incorrectly taps a team member, their team loses a point.

14. When the round is done, every student slides one seat closer to the "prize."

15. The student who was sitting next to the prize gets up and becomes the coin reader, the seat next to the teacher.

16. Repeat until everyone has a chance to be a Coin Reader.

Reflection: What is the relationship between integrity and rules?

Homework: Notice when people follow and don't follow rules.

LESSON 36: Keeping Your Word

Lesson Overview:

Activities in this Lesson:	About These Activities:
Opening Question	Considers the importance of keeping your word.
Your Word	Explores the importance of doing what you say you are going to do.
Trust Walk	Is an experiential exercise that melds integrity with trust and being trustworthy.
Making Things Right	Examines what to do when someone doesn't act with integrity and wants to repair a relationship.

SEL Standards: Responsible Decision-Making / Social Awareness

SEL Objectives: Ethical Responsibility / Respect for Others

ACTIVITY 1: Opening Question

Time: 5 mins

Ask: "Share an experience in which someone did what they said they were going to do or share when someone did not do what they said they were going to do."

ACTIVITY 2: Your Word

Time: 5–10 mins

Instructions:

1. Say, "One version of integrity is doing what you said you were going to do."

2. Ask, "How does it feel when someone does what they say they were going to do?"

3. Ask, "How does it feel when someone doesn't do what they say they were going to do?"

4. Ask, "What gets in the way of people doing what they say they are going to do?"

Reflection: Why is keeping your word important?

ACTIVITY 3: Trust Walk

Time: 15–25 mins

Instructions:

1. Divide students into pairs.

2. One student will be "Guided" the other student will be the "Guide."

3. The Guide will stand behind the Guided and place their hands on his or her shoulders.

4. The Guided closes their eyes.

5. The Guide will use their hands to move the Guided.

6. The Guide can go in any direction, but most importantly, can stop if there is traffic ahead.

7. The Guide gives the Guided their word that they will move them slowly and safely around the room.

8. After one minute, switch roles.

9. Ask, "What was it like to give your word and live up to it?"

10. Ask, "What can you do when a mistake happens?"

Reflection: How can you be trustworthy?

ACTIVITY 4: Making Things Right

Time: 10–15 mins

Instructions:

1. Ask, "When did you have to apologize to someone or someone had to apologize to you? Did the apology work? Why or why not?"

2. Say, "When you do not live up to/keep your word, follow this 3-part structure to create a quality apology."

   a. Acknowledge the mistake and the impact it had on the other person.

   b. State what you will do differently in the future.

   c. Ask if you can do anything to make the situation right.

3. Give the class a sample apology. Have them rate it on a scale from 1–10.

   Example:

   a. I am sorry you are bothered that I was late.

   b. I am sorry that I ate your cookie. I won't do it again, assuming you don't put another cookie in front of me.

   c. I am sorry for bumping into you, but you were not looking.

   d. Excuse you.

   e. I really messed up by not telling you about the party. I understand that since I didn't say anything, you didn't know about it. I just forgot to mention it, but next time I know something, even if you are not there, I will text you. Are we good? Do you need me to do something else?

Reflection: What's the relationship between trust and giving your word?

Homework: Next time you make a promise/give your word to do something, note whether you keep it.

184

LESSON 37: Excuses

Lesson Overview:

Activities in this Lesson:	About These Activities:
Opening Question	Comically asks students to share bad excuses.
Good and Bad Excuses	Looks at comical reasons we give for not doing things we are supposed to do.
Creative Solutions	Offers a new paradigm for handling obstacles.
Choices	Retrospectively looks at past excuses we have made.

SEL Standards: Self-Awareness / Self-Management

SEL Objectives: Self-Perception / Impulse Control

ACTIVITY 1: Opening Question

Time: 5 mins

Ask: "What is the worst excuse you have ever heard?"

ACTIVITY 2: Good and Bad Excuses

Time: 10–15 mins

Instructions:

1. Ask, "What happens when you give a bad excuse?"

2. Ask, "If the consequence is bad, why do people make bad excuses?"
   Possible Answers:
   a. We do it to avoid punishment;
   b. We have to say something;
   c. A bad excuse is better than admitting you did something wrong;
   d. You are going to be punished anyway.

3. Ask, "What is the difference between a good excuse and a bad excuse?"

4. Share example excuses and have the class decide which ones are good and which are bad.

   Example:

   a. I was late because the bus was late.

   b. I was late because nobody woke me up.

   c. I didn't do my work because I was in the hospital.

   d. I got a bad grade because my teacher doesn't like me.

   e. I lost the game because I am not good at chess.

Reflection: Why is it important to distinguish between a good and bad excuse?

ACTIVITY 3: Creative Solutions

Time: 10–15 mins

Instructions: Say, "Many times, people give up too soon when faced with an obstacle. There is often a solution for every problem if we give ourselves the chance to think creatively. Think of creative solutions for these excuses:

   a. A group member didn't do any work, so our group project got a poor grade.

   b. I didn't work out because the gym was closed for renovations.

   c. I can't go to the movies because I have no money.

   d. I don't have time to do my homework today because I have to clean my house.

Reflection: How does a creative solution show integrity?

ACTIVITY 4: Choices

Time:

10–15 mins

Instructions:

1. Ask, "What was a time that did you not do something you were supposed to do? Or, what was a time you did not do something that you wanted to do? What got in your way?"

2. "What was in your power? What was not in your power?"

3. "Looking back, was there a creative solution?"

4. "If not, was there a way to make the situation right with someone else?"

5. "What happens when you settle for a good excuse, as opposed to finding a creative solution, or owning up to a problem and making it right?"

6. "How do you explain what happened without seeming like you are making excuses?"

Reflections:

- How do excuses hinder effectiveness?

- What would taking responsibility look like in your life?

Homework:

Notice when you make an excuse, and instead take responsibility for the situation.

LESSON 38: Group Integrity

Lesson Overview:

Activities in this Lesson:	About These Activities:
Opening Question	Looks at the effect of integrity on a group.
Ropes Shapes	Makes students aware of the value of group integrity.
Octopus Brain	Enables students to simultaneously think about themselves and others.
Paper Clip Chain	Is a competitive game where success is dependent on every group member giving their best effort.

SEL Standards: Responsible Decision-Making / Relationship Skills

SEL Objectives: Ethical Responsibility / Teamwork

ACTIVITY 1: Opening Question

Time: 5 mins

Ask: "How is the group affected when one person doesn't act with integrity?"

ACTIVITY 2: Rope Shapes

Time: 10–15 mins

Supplies: 6 pieces of rope measuring about 10 ft.

Set up: Create loops with each rope.

Instructions:
1. Divide the class into groups of 4–6 students.
2. Have all students hold onto the rope with one hand.
3. Ask the students to make as many shapes as they can within 5 minutes without any student releasing their hold on the rope.

Reflection: How did everyone's integrity affect the success of the group?

ACTIVITY 3: Octopus Brain

Time: 10–15 mins

Instructions:

1. Divide the class into groups of six to eight students.

2. Share that an octopus has a small brain in each of its eight arms.

3. Ask each student to stack their hands together, one on top of another.

4. Tell students that without talking, one student at a time will lead the group to a spot in the classroom.

5. Switch leadership until everyone has an opportunity to lead.

Reflections:

- What was it like to share leadership?

- What's the relationship between leading, following, and acting with integrity?

ACTIVITY 4: Paper Clip Chain

Time: 10–15 mins

Supplies: 3 boxes of paper clips

Instructions:

1. Divide students into groups of four.

2. Tell students their task is to create the longest chain of paper clips in 5 minutes using only one hand each.

3. At the end of 5 minutes, ask how each group member's integrity affected the success of the group.

4. Have each group disassemble the chains and place all of the paper clips back in the box.

Reflection: What is the best way to create group integrity?

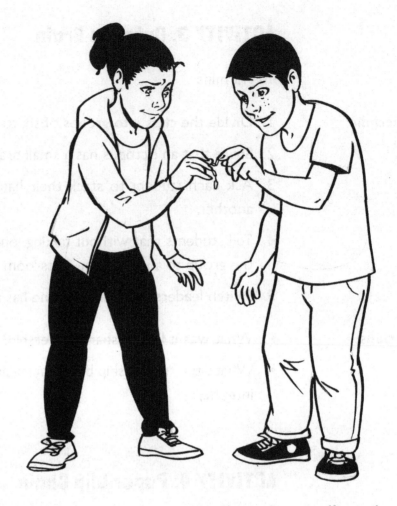

Homework: Notice how and why groups work effectively or ineffectively.

UNIT 8: Mindfulness

▶ Applies breathing techniques to promote self-connection and peace of mind

▶ Engages all five senses to practice mindfulness

▶ Uses self-talk to make empowered decisions

▶ Generates choice for how we perceive the world

LESSON 39: Breath

Lesson Overview:

Activities in this Lesson:	About These Activities:
Opening Question	Introduces breath awareness.
Breathing Techniques	Explores 5 different ways to use our breath to be mindful.
Breath and Focus	Utilizes mindfulness to improve reading skills.

SEL Standards: Self-Awareness

SEL Objectives: Body-Mind Awareness

ACTIVITY 1: Opening Question

Time: 5 mins

Ask: "When do you notice your breath?

ACTIVITY 2: Breathing Techniques

Time: 15–20 mins

Instructions:

1. Ask, "What do you know about Mindfulness?"

2. Share, "The most common mindfulness practice is noticing your breath."

3. Share five different strategies for noticing your breath:

   a. Technique 1: Have students count to 4 as they breath in and count again as they breath out.

   b. Technique 2: Notice when you naturally switch from breathing in to breathing out, and go from breathing out to breathing in.

   c. Technique 3: Place hands on the stomach and notice how the stomach expands with an in-breath, and retracts when breathing out.

   d. Technique 4: Lift the elbows upwards about the inch on the in-breath, relax the elbows on the out-breath.

   e. Technique 5: Ask students to use one finger to slowly trace the outside of the thumb of the opposite hand, starting at the bottom and finishing at the top. As students trace the outside of the thumb, ask them to take a deep breath in. Have students trace the inside of the thumb going top to bottom and ask them to breathe out. As students repeat this instruction with the other fingers, ask them to notice the sensation of physical contact and breath working together.

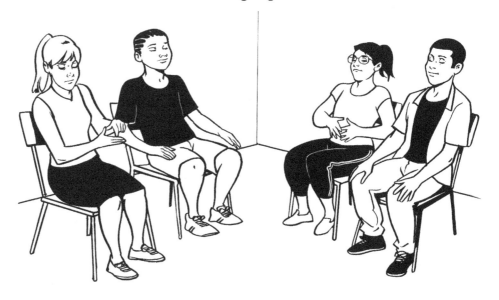

f. For all of these activities, students need to give their attention only to their breath. Tell students that when their minds wander, simply notice the wandering mind, and bring their attention back to breathing.

4. Practice each technique one at a time for one minute.

5. After each practice session, ask students to reflect on their experience.

Reflection: How do your body and mind feel after these activities?

ACTIVITY 3: Breath and Focus

Time: 25 mins

Instructions:

1. Ask students to choose their favorite breathing technique.

2. Tell students they will be interspersing reading for 5 minutes with their favorite technique of mindful breathing. The purpose of the activity is to notice the effects of breathing mindfully.

3. Tell students to read a shared text or independently.

4. After five minutes, tell students to stop reading and use their favorite technique for breathing mindfully for one minute.

5. Tell students to return to reading for five minutes.

6. After five minutes, tell students to stop reading and use the same breathing technique for one minute.

7. Have students read for five minutes one last time.

Variation: Apply the mindfulness practice to a different activity.

Reflection: What impact did mindful breathing have on you?

Homework: Stop and just notice your breath for one minute. Notice what effect this has on you.

LESSON 40: Sensory Mindfulness

Lesson Overview:

Activities in this Lesson:	About These Activities:
Opening Question	Asks students their favorite techniques for being present.
5 Senses Mindfulness	Offers students 5 ways to connect to the present moment.
Rice and Beans Count	Is a tactile mindfulness exercise.

SEL Standards: Self-Awareness

SEL Objectives: Body-Mind Awareness

ACTIVITY 1: Opening Question

Time: 5 mins

Ask: "How do you stay present in the moment?"

ACTIVITY 2: Five Senses Mindfulness

Time: 25 mins

Supplies:
- Flower petals with a strong aroma
- Box of raisins
- Cell phone with a gong sound effect

1. Ask, "What are the five senses?"

2. Explain we are going to practice noticing the present with all of our senses.

3. Explain you are going to ring a gong; when the students can not hear it any more, they should raise their hand.

4. Play the gong sound from your cell phone; repeat when everyone has their hand up.

5. Ask students to share their experience with someone.

6. Have students identify as many blue objects in the room as possible in one minute.

7. Ask students to share their experience with someone.

8. Give a flower petal to each student. Have them notice its smells for thirty seconds and not focus on anything else.

9. Ask students to share their experience with someone.

10. Give each student a raisen to eat. Have them chew it slowly, noticing the texture and flavor.

11. Ask students to share their experience with someone.

12. Stand up and slowly walk around the room, noticing the transfer of weight in their feet, while looking down.

13. Ask students to share their experience with someone.

Reflection: Which sensory exploration helped you feel more present?

ACTIVITY 3: Rice and Beans Count

Time: 10–15 mins

Supplies:
- 3 pounds of dried rice
- 3 pounds of dried beans
- 6 cloth or paper bags

Instructions:
1. Pour an equal amount of rice and beans into each bag.
2. Divide the class into six groups.
3. Give each group a bag.

4. Ask each group to silently and slowly separate the beans from the grains of rice.

5. Ask students to bring their attention to the feeling of beans in their hands.

6. Ask students to notice their breath as they do this task.

7. Tell students that if the mind wanders, ask students to simply return to their breath and task at hand.

8. After five minutes, have them put the rice and beans back into the bag.

9. Ask, "How did you feel before, during, and after this activity?"

10. Ask, "How does focusing on simple actions affect you?"

11. Ask, "What was it like to mix the rice and beans at the end of the activity after separating them?"

Reflection: What did you learn about being present?

Homework: For one minute, stop and focus on the present moment using one of your five senses.

LESSON 41: Self-Talk

Lesson Overview:

Activities in this Lesson:	About These Activities:
Opening Question	Asks students to share what they think about.
Noticing Your Thinking	Asks students to be mindful of their thoughts.
Problem Solving Self-Talk	Empowers students to notice what they are thinking when they approach a problem.

SEL Standards: Self-Awareness

SEL Objectives: Self-Perception

ACTIVITY 1: Opening Question

Time: 5 mins

Ask: "What topics do you think or daydream about most often?"

ACTIVITY 2: Noticing Your Thinking

Time: 20 mins

Instructions:

1. Say, "Part of mindfulness is noticing what arises without judgment. We are going to do some exercises to notice what comes up in our minds."

2. Ask students to sit still and be silent and observe what they are thinking about for one minute. They don't have to try to do anything with their thoughts. Their task is to just notice.

3. After one minute, ask students to share with someone what they were thinking about.

4. Divide students into pairs.

5. Have Student A notice and share whatever is on their mind in one minute, filtering only what is private or inappropriate. Student B just listens.

6. Have Student A and Student B switch roles.

7. Read aloud any fiction or nonfiction text. Ask students to track what thoughts arise in their minds as they listen.

8. Demonstrate noticing everything you think about as you read a passage aloud, including questions, inferences, and when your mind wanders.

9. Provide an engaging text for students to read.

10. Have Student A read aloud a different passage and share what they are thinking about as they read. Student B just listens.

11. Switch roles.

12. Ask, "What did you notice about your thoughts?"

ACTIVITY 3: Problem Solving Self-Talk

Time: 20 mins

Supplies: Masking tape

Instructions:

1. Say, "We are going to bring awareness to what we think about as we come across a problem."

2. Divide students into three groups.

3. Mark off a row of tiles or apply 10 feet of masking tape.

4. Have one group step on that row of tiles or masking tape.

5. Explain that their challenge is to reverse the order of the group in the line without stepping outside the row of tiles, or by stepping outside the line of tape.

6. If anyone steps outside the row of tiles, or off the tape, the whole process starts from the beginning.

7. Let students know they will have 10 minutes to complete the task.

8. Ask students to notice what they are thinking as they try to accomplish this task.

9. Throughout the activity, remind students to notice what they are thinking.

10. After 10 minutes, stop and have students share what they noticed about their thinking.

Reflection: What type of thoughts did you become aware of?

Homework: Bring awareness to your thinking throughout the day.

LESSON 42: Mindfulness...Now What?

Lesson Overview:

Activities in this Lesson:	About These Activities:
Opening Question	Asks students to think about how to apply their mindfulness skills.
Focus	Reveals the power of focus.
Two Circles	Offers students a choice about where to place their focus.
Tangrams	Is a group challenge which allows students to focus on the possibility of success.

SEL Standards: Self-Awareness

SEL Objectives: Self-Perception

ACTIVITY 1: Opening Question

Time: 5 mins

Ask: "How can you use your mindfulness skills?"

ACTIVITY 2: Focus

Time: 10–15 mins

Instructions: 1. Ask students to look around the room and find as many things with the color red as possible in thirty seconds.

2. After thirty seconds, tell students to share what they saw with someone next to them.

3. Ask students to look around the room and notice as many things that are circular as possible in thirty seconds.

4. After thirty seconds, tell students to share what they saw with someone next to them.

5. Ask, "How many red things did you notice? How many circular objects did you notice?"

6. Ask, "What can we conclude from this activity?" (When we decide to look for something, we are more likely to see it.)

Reflections:

- How does focus affect what we see and notice?

- How can we use this knowledge to improve our lives?

ACTIVITY 3: Two Circles

Time: 15–20 mins

Supplies: A copy of the Native American legend "Two Wolves."

Instructions:

1. Draw two large circles.

2. Say, "Think about a goal you have that you haven't been able to achieve."

3. Ask, "Why haven't you been able to achieve it?"

4. Write down responses in one circle.

5. After filling the circle, say, "Notice what you feel right now about accomplishing a goal."

6. Ask, "Think about ways you still can achieve this goal, despite a lack of past success."

7. Write these responses in the other circle.

8. After filling the second circle, say, "Notice what you feel right now about accomplishing your goal."

9. Ask, "What can you conclude after doing this activity?"

10. Read the Native American legend, "Two Wolves."

11. Say, "Our thoughts arise in our minds as if they are an accurate description of the world as it is. However, there are many ways to interact with the world and we get to choose the prism through which we see it."

12. Ask, "How do you see the world and how does that affect the way you experience it?"

13. Ask, "Once we become aware of our thoughts, what can we do with them?

    Potential Answers:

    a. Be curious about them,

    b. Evaluate their utility,

    c. Notice and release them,

    d. Connect them to what we are feeling and needing,

    e. Reconnect to an intention that matches our goal or values.

Reflection: How can you apply the lesson from "Two Wolves" to your life?

ACTIVITY 4: Tangrams

Time: 15–20 mins

Supplies: • 10 Sets of tangrams (purchase or create them)

                   • 10 Tangram Shape Handout

                   A full size version of this worksheet is available in the appendix.

⊠ **TANGRAM WITH LINES**

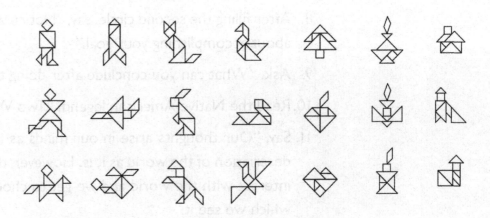

■ TANGRAM SILHOUETTES

Instructions:

1. Divide the class into groups of 3–4 students.

2. Give each group a tangram set and the Tangram Shape Handout.

3. Say, "For round one, use the top half of the Tangram Shape Handout to make as many shapes as you can within 2 minutes."

4. Give groups 2 minutes to come up with as many shapes as they can.

5. Tally the results.

6. Ask students to notice their thinking and whether their thoughts are helping them or not helping.

   If their thoughts are not helping them, ask them to focus on the possibility of being successful.

7. Say, "For round two, you will have another 2 minutes to make as many shapes as you can using the top half of the Tangram Shape Handout. Notice your thoughts and consider the possibility you will be successful."

8. Give the groups another 2 minutes to come up with as many shapes as they can.

9. Compare the results.

Variation: For a third round, use the bottom half of the Tangram Shape Handout to make as many shapes as possible within 5 minutes. These shapes do not show which Tangrams to use. The task will be more difficult. Ask students to notice their thoughts and consider the possibility they will be successful.

Reflection: How did your awareness of your thoughts influence your productivity?

Homework: Notice what you are thinking about as you approach an obstacle.

210

UNIT 9: Goal Setting

▶ Creates specific and measurable goals

▶ Divides goals into attainable steps

▶ Brainstorms creative solutions to overcome obstacles

▶ Explores inner and outer motivation

LESSON 43: Starting with Goals

Lesson Overview:

Activities in this Lesson:	About These Activities:
Opening Question	Reflects on successful experiences with setting goals.
Goal Planning	Has students brainstorm what they want in life.
SMART Goals	Asks students to make their goals specific and measurable.
Goal Declaration	Makes students' goals more accountable by sharing them with the community.

SEL Standards: Self-Management

SEL Objectives: Goal Setting

ACTIVITY 1: Opening Question

Time: 5 mins

Ask: "What is a goal you had that you were able to achieve?"

ACTIVITY 2: Goal Planning

Time: 15–20 mins

Supplies: Class set of Mind Map worksheets

A full size version of this worksheet is available in the appendix.

NAME - ....

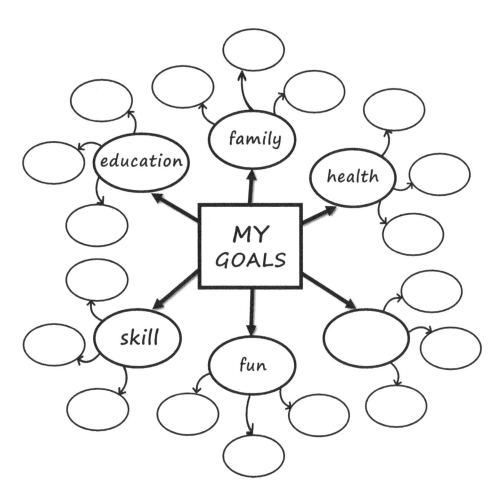

Instructions:

1. Say, "We are going to study how to achieve what we want in life."

2. Ask, "What is something you want? Nothing is too small or too big. It could be world peace, an extra plate of spaghetti, or a better math grade."

3. Give a copy of the Mind map to each student.

4. Say, "We are going to use the Mind Map to brainstorm ideas for what you want. Use the categories to think about different areas of your life. Even if you think of a goal that seems unattainable, write it down."

5. Say, "Be as specific as possible. If you are struggling thinking of goals, it's okay to think of things you don't want in your life. This will lead you to what you want."

6. Give students 10 minutes to fill out the Mind Map.

7. Ask students to choose an easy goal they can start working on in this unit of study.

Reflection: What does it feel like to think about all the things you want in life?

ACTIVITY 3: SMART Goals

Time: 15–20 mins

Instructions:

1. Say, "It is now time to transform your goal into a SMART goal. A SMART goal is an acronym that stands for specific, measurable, attainable, relevant, and timed. SMART goals help you be clear about what you want and track how close you are to getting it."

2. Say, "S stands for SPECIFIC. Being specific gives you a clear target to focus on. In order to be specific, think of the details of your goal."

   For Example:

   a. Instead of saying "I want to make money," it's more specific to say "I want to earn $50 a week."

   b. Instead of wanting to spend more time with a parent, think of what you would want to do with them. A movie? A concert? A game?

3. Say, "M stands for MEASURABLE. It's crucial to measure your goals so you know whether you are making progress or not."

   For Example:

   a. If you want to get stronger, how many more push ups and sit ups do you want to do?

   b. If you want to learn a new language, how many words do you want to learn each day?

4. Say, "A stands for ATTAINABLE: Is the goal within reach or is it impossible to achieve? Can you reshape the goal so that you are able to achieve it? Can you alter your goal so you can take the first steps towards reaching your goal?"

   For Example:

   a. If your goal is to end world hunger, maybe revise your goal to start a food drive at your school.

   b. If your goal is to be the best gamer within a week, you could revise your goal to being the best among your friends in a week.

215

5. Say, "R stands for RELEVANT: Is your goal connected to things you are passionate about? Is your goal connected to values that are important to you?"

For Example:

a. If creativity is important to you, important to you, try setting a goal to learn how to play an instrument.

b. If fashion is important to you, you could organize a fashion show.

My goal: _____

SPECIFIC	Narrow down a larger desire into specific details. What is my target?	
MEASURABLE	What milestones can I set? How can I track my progress?	
ATTAINABLE	Is my goal realistic and reachable? How can I make it possible to achieve?	
RELEVANT	Why this goal? Why is this important to me?	
TIMED	Do I have a deadline? When do I want to reach my goal?	

6. Say, "T stands for TIMED: Does your goal have a deadline? Depending on what you want to achieve, the deadline could be 24 hours, next week, or next month."

   For Example:

   a. If your goal is to learn how to salsa dance, take a class every Thursday for 4 weeks.

   b. If your goal is to cook dinner for your family, choose a day and time each week you want to commit to doing it.

7. Say, "Now, using these concepts, transform your easy goal into a SMART goal. Make sure your goal meets all the criteria for a SMART goal."

   A full size version of this worksheet is available in the appendix.

Reflection: How can SMART goals help you achieve what you want?

ACTIVITY 4: Goal Declaration

Time: 10 mins

Instructions: 1. Have each student go around the room and declare one SMART goal that they will complete by the next class.

                    2. Have students share one action they will take towards their goal.

Reflection: What did you learn about achieving a goal?

Homework: Take one action towards your goal.

LESSON 44: Step by Step

Lesson Overview:

Activities in this Lesson:	About These Activities:
Opening Question	Asks students for a status update with their goals.
Step by Step Map	Helps students break down their goals into steps.
Juggling Scarves	Is a captivating activity to practice achieving goals with support

SEL Standards: Responsible Decision-Making

SEL Objectives: Analyzing Problems and Brainstorming Solutions

ACTIVITY 1: Opening Question

Time: 5 mins

Ask: "Did you make progress towards your goal? Why or why not?"

ACTIVITY 2: Step by Step Map

Time: 20–25 mins

Instructions: 1. Ask, "How do you climb a mountain?"

2. Say, " One step at a time. If you dwell on the length of a journey, it can seem overwhelming. However, when you break a goal down into smaller parts, step by step, each part becomes more manageable."

3. Say, "Brainstorm as many steps as possible to achieve your goal on the Step by Step worksheet.

   A full size version of this worksheet is available in the appendix.

   Sample:

   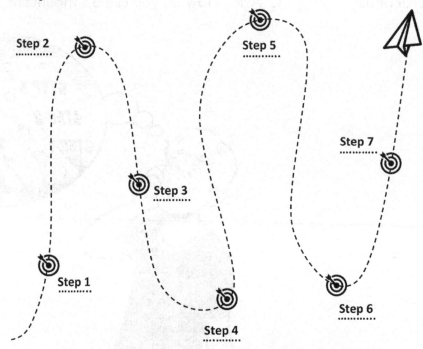

   Here are some questions to help you create smaller steps:

   a. Question 1: What actions do you need to take in order to achieve your goal? Be as specific as possible.

   b. Question 2: What skills do you still need to learn and practice to achieve your goal? Is there more than one? Which skills do you need to learn first?

   c. Question 3: What, or whose, help do you need to achieve these skills? What steps do you need to take to get help?

   d. Question 4: What timeframe does your goal require? List the different segments of time as steps towards your goal.

4. Have students do a gallery walk to view everyone's step by step worksheet.

Reflection: What is the value of breaking up a goal into steps?

ACTIVITY 3: Juggling Scarves

Time:

15–20 mins

Supplies:

- 2 class sets of juggling scarves

- A bag for all the scarves

Instructions:

1. Say, "Learning how to juggle requires many steps and lots of practice before you are proficient. We are going to practice the step by step concept by learning to juggle scarves."

2. Show a video *Scarf Juggling Basics* about juggling scarves on YouTube: *https://www.youtube.com/watch?v=ve2FKNctOBg*

3. Place the juggling scarves in a bag.

4. Divide the class into two groups, Group A and Group B.

5. Match one student from Group A with one student from Group B.

6. Tell Student A they will practice for 2 minutes, while Student B offers support and coaching. Then the students will switch roles.

7. Have Group A take one scarf out of the bag to start.

Reflection: What steps will you take between now and next class to achieve your goal?

Homework: Take a few steps towards your goal.

LESSON 45: Creative Solutions

Lesson Overview:

Activities in this Lesson:	About These Activities:
Opening Question	Asks students to share the ups and downs of pursuing their goal.
Traffic Jam	Presents an opportunity to practice problem solving as a group.
Blanket Flip	Is an opportunity for problem solving when a solution may seem impossible.
Obstacles and Creative Solutions	Reflectively looks at applying creative solutions to one's obstacles.

SEL Standards: Responsible Decision-Making / Relationship Skills

SEL Objectives: Analyzing Problems and Brainstorming Solutions, Teamwork

ACTIVITY 1: Opening Question

Time: 5 mins

Ask: "What successes and what challenges did you encounter trying to achieve your goal?"

ACTIVITY 2: Traffic Jam

Time: 15–20 mins

Supplies: 7 hula hoops

Instructions:

1. Ask, "How did you handle obstacles that got in the way of your goal?"

2. Ask, "Did anyone have an obstacle they could not overcome?"

3. Ask the class for creative solutions to everyone's obstacles.

4. Say, "When there is a problem, sometimes there is no solution, but often there is. We simply need to try something different, better, or get help being creative."

5. Say, "We are going to play a game called Traffic Jam. The task will seem impossible. We will practice not giving up and being creative with solutions."

6. Ask for six volunteers for the game. Everyone who doesn't play can offer ideas to help solve the problem.

7. Lay out seven hula hoops in a line.

8. Keep the middle hula hoop open.

9. Have the students stand in the other spots and face each other. Explain that for this challenge, both sides of the line must switch their order. However:

   a. Only one student can move at a time.

224

b. Only one student is on each spot at a time.

c. Students can't move backwards.

d. A student can't go around or jump over a teammate in front of them.

10. If two players are facing each other, Student A can move around Student B only if there is an empty space behind Student B.

11. If there is a traffic jam, everyone has to start again.

Reflection: What did you learn about solving problems?

ACTIVITY 3: Blanket Flip

Time: 15–20 mins

Supplies: A large sheet or blanket

Instructions: 1. Divide the class into four groups.

2. Give each group a sheet or blanket to stand on.

3. Have the entire group stand on the edges of the blanket.

4. Challenge the group to completely flip it over so everyone will be standing on the other side of the blanket.

5. No one is allowed to step off the blanket.

Reflection: How can you apply what you learned about solving problems to other situations in life?

ACTIVITY 4: Obstacles and Creative Solutions

Time: 5–10 mins

Instructions:
1. Ask, "What could be a creative solution to an obstacle you faced when trying to achieve your goal?"

2. Ask, "What obstacles could you face in the future?"

3. Ask, "What creative solutions can you come up with to overcome these obstacles?"

Reflection: How can creative solutions help you in your life?

Homework: Notice how you react to an obstacle and seek a creative solution.

LESSON 46: Increasing the Possibility for Success

Lesson Overview:

Activities in this Lesson:	About These Activities:
Opening Question	Asks what is personally motivating.
Motivation and Inspiration	Explores internal approaches for attaining one's goals.
Celebrations	Examines the importance of celebrations on the path toward achieving one's goals.
Feather Balancing	Tantalizingly challenges and opportunity to practice internal and external motivation.

SEL Standards: Self-Management

SEL Objectives: Self-Motivation

ACTIVITY 1: Opening Question

Time: 5 mins

Ask: "How do you motivate yourself?"

ACTIVITY 2: Motivation and Inspiration

Time:

15–20 mins

Instructions:

1. Ask, "What motivates and inspires you?"

2. Ask, "How can you motivate and inspire yourself as you attempt to achieve your goal?"

3. Say, "Many people press the snooze button again and again. The temptation to get a little more rest is too strong. You keep pressing snooze until you show up to school late. One thing you can do is place your alarm clock across the room. Then you have to get out of bed in order to turn the sound off. Once you get out of bed, you often won't go back to sleep. *By setting up your environment to support your ultimate goal, you have a better chance at success.*"

4. Ask, "How can you set your environment up for success?"

5. Ask, "What distracts you?"

6. Ask, "How can you change your environment so that you don't get distracted? Can you turn your phone off when you are working on a project? If you have friends who distract you, can you inform them when it is ok and not ok to message you?

7. Tell students to create a T-chart.

   a. Left side: What commonly distracts from achieving your goal?

   b. Right side: How can you change your environment to lessen the impact of those distractions?

Reflection:

What are the best ways for you to increase your motivation and decrease your distractions?

ACTIVITY 3: Celebrations

Time: 5–10 mins

Instructions:
1. Ask, "What is the importance of celebration?"

2. Ask, "How do you celebrate your successes?"

3. Ask, "Do you believe in waiting until the end of the journey or do you have mini celebrations along the way? Why or why not?"

Reflection: What celebrations will you plan during or after you achieve your goal?

ACTIVITY 4: Feather Balancing

Time: 15–20 mins

Supplies: A class set of feathers

Instructions:
1. Say, "We are going to try to balance a feather for one minute using only the tip of one finger. Think about what would increase your possibility of success. Think about how celebration might play a role in your process."
2. Give a feather to each student.
3. Give students 10 mins to practice.

Reflection: What helped and what did not help your feather balancing attempts?

Homework: Change your environment to increase the possibility of achieving your goal.

UNIT 10: Resilience

▶ Teaches tools for perseverance and grit

▶ Uses failure as a learning opportunity

▶ Examines the role of beliefs in achieving success

▶ Celebrates the value of practice

LESSON 47: Bouncing Back

Lesson Overview:

Activities in this Lesson:	About These Activities:
Opening Question	Asks students to share their experiences with struggle.
Maze	Challenges students to be resilient in the face of choosing the wrong path.

SEL Standards: Responsible Decision-Making

SEL Objectives: Analyzing Problems and Brainstorming Solutions

ACTIVITY 1: Opening Question

Time: 5 mins

Ask: "How do you deal with struggle?"

ACTIVITY 2: Maze

Time: 40 mins

Supplies: Masking tape

Instructions: 1. Say, "Resilience is the capacity to recover from difficulties."

2. Ask, "When is it important to be resilient?"

3. Say, "We are going to do an activity to test our ability to be resilient."

4. Make a 4′ by 4′ grid with masking tape (or if there is a tile floor, mark off a 4 tiles by 4 tiles).

5. The squares should be large enough for two feet.

6. Divide students into three groups of 7–10 students.

7. Have one group at a time try to cross the grid within 5 minutes. To cross the grid successfully, the group must follow a secret walking pattern/combination.

8. Let students know there are no diagonals and they never step into the same box twice.

9. Create a secret walking pattern/combination/maze for students to follow.

10. Students in group A line up one by one to try crossing the square.

11. Students in group B and C watch.

a. If the box is part of the walking pattern, say nothing (the silence is part of the drama). If the box is not correct, make a buzzer sound.

b. If the student steps into the correct square, they can proceed to another square.

c. If they step into the wrong square, they must go to the back of the line in their group and wait their turn to start again.

12. When one student makes it across the square, the next student must successfully repeat the same walking pattern.

13. If any successive student steps into the wrong box, all the students have to go back and start again.

14. The game ends when all members of the group make it to the other side.

15. After group A finishes, mark their time.

16. Repeat with a Group B and C with new walking patterns.

Reflection: What did you learn about learning from mistakes?

Homework: Note how you handle difficulty.

LESSON 48: Growth Mindset

Lesson Overview:

Activities in this Lesson:	About These Activities:
Opening Question	Juxtaposes talent and effort.
Growth Mindset vs. Fixed Mindset	Powerfully reframes our mental approach to tasks.
Growth Mindset Practice	Uses a carnival game to encourage students to use a growth mindset.

SEL Standards: Self-Awareness

SEL Objectives: Self-Perception

ACTIVITY 1: Opening Questions

Time: 5 mins

Ask: "What percentage of success is due to talent? What percentage is due to effort?"

ACTIVITY 2: Growth Mindset vs. Fixed Mindset

Time:

20 mins

Instructions:

1. Say, "Our ideas about learning can change the way we learn and deal with difficulty. Your beliefs influence what you do. Psychologist Carol Dweck coined the term "growth mindset" to help people think in a new way about the possibilities for learning new skills, developing their intelligence, and handling struggle."

2. Show the YouTube video, "Growth Mindset vs. Fixed Mindset." *https://www.youtube.com/watch?v=MICHPnZfFmU*

3. Ask, "When you are learning, do you use the growth mindset or a fixed mindset?"

4. Ask the class to change these fixed mindset statements into growth mindset statements:

   a. I'm terrible at science.

   b. I hope nobody noticed my mistake.

   c. This is too difficult.

   d. I don't know how to do this; I'm out of here!

   e. Other people must do this naturally.

   f. I am perfect.

   g. I hate challenges.

   h. I either know it or I don't.

   i. He's smarter. I'm never going to be that smart.

   j. It's good enough.

Reflection:

How can a growth mindset benefit you?

ACTIVITY 3: Growth Mindset Practice

Time:

20 mins

236

Supplies: 6 bean bag toss games

Instructions:

1. Say, "Using the growth mindset, we are going to practice throwing bean bags underhand"

2. Ask, "If you are *not* successful, using a growth mindset, how can you approach the challenge."

3. Ask, "If you are successful, how can you use a growth mindset to continue to challenge yourself?"

4. Divide the class into six groups and set up a bean bag toss for each group.

5. Ask students to take turns tossing the bean bags. Students should notice their thoughts and use a growth mindset.

Reflection: How can a growth mindset help you learn?

Homework: Notice when you are thinking with a growth mindset or a fixed mindset.

LESSON 49: Beliefs

Lesson Overview:

Activities in this Lesson:	About These Activities:
Opening Question	Introduces the topic of beliefs and their connection to success.
Beliefs in Action	Has students examine their beliefs when facing a difficult task.
Wire Puzzles	Gives students a second opportunity to look at their beliefs when trying to accomplish that seems impossible.

SEL Standards: Self-Awareness

SEL Objectives: Self-Perception

ACTIVITY 1: Opening Question

Time: 5 mins

Ask: "What do people need to believe in order to be successful?"

ACTIVITY 2: Beliefs in Action

Time: 20 mins

Supplies:	15 plastic water bottles ⅓ full
Instructions:	1. Ask, "How does what you believe affect your resilience?"

Supplies: 15 plastic water bottles ⅓ full

Instructions:

1. Ask, "How does what you believe affect your resilience?"

2. Say, "Beliefs are feelings of certainty about the world. They communicate to us what is possible and what isn't. It can be useful to notice what we believe and how our beliefs influence what we do."

3. Show a compilation of water bottle challenges *Top 100 Ultimate Water Bottle Flip Challenge Compilation Videos* from YouTube. *https://www.youtube.com/watch?v=Kp5QMSbf-a0&t=208s*

4. Ask, "How do we reevaluate a belief that a task is impossible?"

5. Ask, "When something seems impossible, how do you cultivate hope?"

6. Divide students into pairs.

7. Give each pair one water bottle to practice with.

8. Say, "As you attempt the water bottle challenge, notice what you believe and how it affects your actions and results."

Reflections:

• How did your beliefs about what was possible affect your action?

• How did your partner's beliefs / ideas about success impact your actions and results?

ACTIVITY 3: Wire Puzzles

Time: 20 mins

Supplies: 4 boxes containing 8 wire puzzles

Instructions:
1. Set up 8 stations, each with the same type of puzzles.
2. Divide the class into 8 groups.
3. Tell students they will have 5 minutes in each station to try to separate the pieces.
4. After 5 minutes, rotate the groups to the next station.

Reflection: How do you create hope when things seem impossible?

Homework: Notice what you believe about a task as you do it.

LESSON 50: Practice

Lesson Overview:

Activities in this Lesson:	About These Activities:
Opening Question	Considers the role of practice in our life.
Numbers Search	Demonstrates the importance of repeating an activity.
River Crossing	Challenges students to be resilient when faced with difficulty.

SEL Standards: Responsible Decision-Making / Relationship Skills

SEL Objectives: Analyzing Problems and Brainstorming Solutions / Teamwork

ACTIVITY 1: Opening Question

Time: 5 mins

Ask: "What is your relationship with practice?"

ACTIVITY 2: Numbers Search

Time: 20 mins

Supplies: 10 copies of "Numbers Worksheet"

A full size version of this worksheet is available in the appendix.

11 3 50 21 72 33 5 91
93 42 61 35 86 29 18 40
                                23
31 9 95 14 55 78 45 58
                              65
37 2 71 99 77 39
4 56
44 25 49 20 83 28 52
27 70
84 16 89 34 98 79 68
19 57
7 80 53 69 41 17
38 62 73
47 30 74 97 87 24 96
22 6
90 63 48 36
51 32 81 59 100 43 1
15 60 92 76 82
10 75 66 88 85
46 13 67
64 12 94 8 54 26

Instructions:	1. Ask, "What is the relationship between resilience and practice?"
	2. Say, "We are going to do an activity that illustrates the value of practice."
	3. Divide the class into groups of 4 or 5 students.
	4. Give each group a copy of the "Numbers Worksheet" facedown on a desk.
	5. Ask students not to touch it until instructed.
	6. Let the students know there are 100 numbers randomly scattered on a "Numbers Worksheet."
	7. Their task is to find as many numbers in succession as possible, starting with the number 1.
	8. When someone in the group finds a number, they should point at it, and then look for the next number.
	9. Let the students know they will have 2 minutes to do this task.
	10. Start the timer and say, "Go."
	11. At the end of 2 minutes, have each group report what number they were able to reach and reflect on the experience.
	12. Repeat the activity and compare the results.
Reflection:	What did you learn about the value of repeating an activity?

ACTIVITY 3: River Crossing

Time:	20 mins
Supplies:	6-inch cardboard squares
Instructions:	1. Divide students into two groups behind a starting line.
	2. Establish a finish line on the other side of the room.

3. Explain there is a river flowing between the starting and finish lines.

4. Place cardboard squares in between the starting and finish lines as islands.

5. The groups will be competing against each other.

6. The Islands offer both groups equal opportunity to get across the classroom using separate pathways.

7. If students step off the Islands, everyone in the group must go back to the starting line.

8. The challenge is that students have to cross while the outside of one foot stays connected to another student.

9. If any feet become disconnected, the whole group has to start again.

10. After one group wins, ask, "What did this activity teach us about practice?"

Reflection: What are the benefits of practice? What makes practice difficult?

Homework: Notice your thinking as you practice a skill.

244

CONCLUSION

Social emotional learning is the most profound and rewarding work I have done in my teaching career and I am confident that you will treasure it as well. The journey is rich with meaningful opportunities for growth that will last a lifetime. These 50 lessons provide crucial tools that will powerfully impact your students and classrooms. Students will feel more connected, be more social, and they will be able navigate the ups and downs of life with agency and hope.

I wish you all the best on your SEL adventures. Please contact me with any questions or feedback at *info@brooklynSEL.com*. I am excited to hear about your experience and look forward to building our SEL community.

For more information go to
BrooklynSEL.com
DavidParisBooks.com

ABOUT THE AUTHOR

David Paris is an educational consultant with Dance Communication Educators and Director of Social Emotional Learning at Middle School 88 in Brooklyn. He has 30 years of experience teaching in NYC public schools and is a Teach For America alumni. He has authored four adolescent fiction books and founded the Life Goals in the Classroom curriculum. He is a group facilitator of Non-Violent Communication (NYCNVC.ORG) and a trainer with Alternative to Violence Program (AVPUSA.Org). In his spare time, David teaches and performs acrobatics and dance. David is a seven-time acrobatic dance champion, co-director of Paradizo Dance, and was a finalist on America's Got Talent.

APPENDIX

HUMAN SCAVENGER HUNT!!!

Has a pet other than a dog or cat	ENJOYS DANCING	HAS THEIR OWN YOUTUBE CHANNEL	Has a name longer than 6 letters	Speaks another language
-----------------	-----------------	-----------------	-----------------	-----------------
Is left-handed	**Favorite color is purple**	Loves Math	**Plays an instrument**	Likes vegetables
-----------------	-----------------	-----------------	-----------------	-----------------
Enjoys cooking	Likes talking in front of groups	Has a birthday in the same month	USES SAME BRAND OF TOOTH-PASTE	LIKES THE SAME VIDEO GAME
-----------------	-----------------	-----------------	-----------------	-----------------
Same taste in shoes	**Loves snow**	HAS BROKEN A BONE	**Has won an award**	**Exercises every day**
-----------------	-----------------	-----------------	-----------------	-----------------
Walks to school	**Likes the same music you do**	Does not like pizza	Can make a scary face	Likes to repair things
-----------------	-----------------	-----------------	-----------------	-----------------

☺ Feelings Associated with Met Needs ☺

Excited → **Excited**	**Happy** → **Happy**	**Hopeful** → **Hopeful**
Energetic 1) _____	Blissful 1) _____	Confident 1) _____
Enthusiastic 2) _____	Delighted 2) _____	Expectant 2) _____
Passionate 3) _____	Joyful 3) _____	Light hearted 3) _____
Surprised 4) _____	Pleased 4) _____	Upbeat 4) _____

Inspired → **Inspired**	**Interested** → **Interested**	**Peaceful** → **Peaceful**
Amazed 1) _____	Curious 1) _____	Refreshed 1) _____
Motivated 2) _____	Enchanted 2) _____	Relaxed 2) _____
Psyched 3) _____	Fascinated 3) _____	Relieved 3) _____
Stirred 4) _____	Intrigued 4) _____	Satisfied 4) _____

☹ Feelings Associated with Unmet Needs ☹

Anger → **Anger**	**Bored** → **Bored**	**Confused** → **Confused**
Aggravated 1) _____	Apathetic 1) _____	Dazed 1) _____
Annoyed 2) _____	Disconnected 2) _____	Mixed 2) _____
Enraged 3) _____	Distant 3) _____	Mystified 3) _____
Frustrated 4) _____	Numb 4) _____	Torn 4) _____

Disgust → **Disgust**	**Fatigue** → **Fatigue**	**Fear** → **Fear**
Bothered 1) _____	Burnt out 1) _____	Nervous 1) _____
Dislike 2) _____	Sleepy 2) _____	Panicked 2) _____
Horrified 3) _____	Tired 3) _____	Scared 3) _____
Repulsed 4) _____	Weary 4) _____	Worried 4) _____

Pain → **Pain**	**Sadness** → **Sadness**	**Uneasy** → **Uneasy**
Aching 1) _____	Depressed 1) _____	Disturbed 1) _____
Agony 2) _____	Disappointed 2) _____	Embarrassed 2) _____
Hurting 3) _____	Hopeless 3) _____	Uncomfortable 3) _____
Lonely 4) _____	Miserable 4) _____	Upset 4) _____

Feelings Associated with Met Needs

Excited	**Happy**	**Hopeful**
Energetic	Blissful	Confident
Enthusiastic	Delighted	Expectant
Passionate	Joyful	Light hearted
Surprised	Pleased	Upbeat
Inspired	**Interested**	**Peaceful**
Amazed	Curious	Refreshed
Motivated	Enchanted	Relaxed
Psyched	Fascinated	Relieved
Stirred	Intrigued	Satisfied

Feelings Associated with Unmet Needs

Anger	**Bored**	**Confused**
Aggravated	Apathetic	Dazed
Annoyed	Disconnected	Mixed
Enraged	Distant	Mystified
Frustrated	Numb	Torn
Disgust	**Fatigue**	**Fear**
Bothered	Burnt out	Nervous
Dislike	Sleepy	Panicked
Horrified	Tired	Scared
Repulsed	Weary	Worried
Pain	**Sadness**	**Uneasy**
Aching	Depressed	Disturbed
Agony	Disappointed	Embarrassed
Hurting	Hopeless	Uncomfortable
Lonely	Miserable	Upset

*This list is modified from a Feelings List by NYCNVC.

AUTONOMY
Choice
Dignity
Freedom
Independence
Self-expression
Space
Spontaneity

CONNECTION
Acceptance
Affection
Appreciation
Authenticity
Belonging
Care
Closeness
Communication
Communion
Community
Companionship
Compassion
Consideration
Empathy
Friendship
Inclusion
Inspiration
Integrity
Intimacy
Love
Mutuality
Nurturing
Partnership
Presence
Respect/Self-respect
Security
Self-acceptance
Self-care

CONNECTION (cont.)
Self-connection
Self-expression
Shared Reality
Stability
Support
To know and be known
To see and be seen
Trust
Understanding
Warmth

MEANING
Awareness
Celebration
Challenge
Clarity
Competence
Consciousness
Contribution
Creativity
Discovery
Efficiency
Effectiveness
Growth
Integration
Integrity
Learning
Mourning
Movement
Participation
Perspective
Presence
Progress
Purpose
Self-expression
Understanding

PEACE
Acceptance
Balance
Beauty
Ease
Faith
Harmony
Hope
Order
Peace-of-mind
Space

PHYSICAL WELL-BEING
Air
Care
Comfort
Food
Movement/Exercise
Rest/Sleep
Safety
Self-care
Shelter
Water

PLAY
Adventure
Excitement
Fun
Humor
Joy
Relaxation

* This list is modified from a Needs List by NYCNVC

⊠ TANGRAM WITH LINES

■ TANGRAM SILHOUETTES

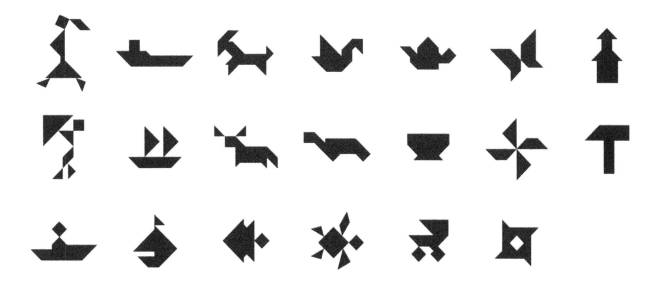

NAME - ....

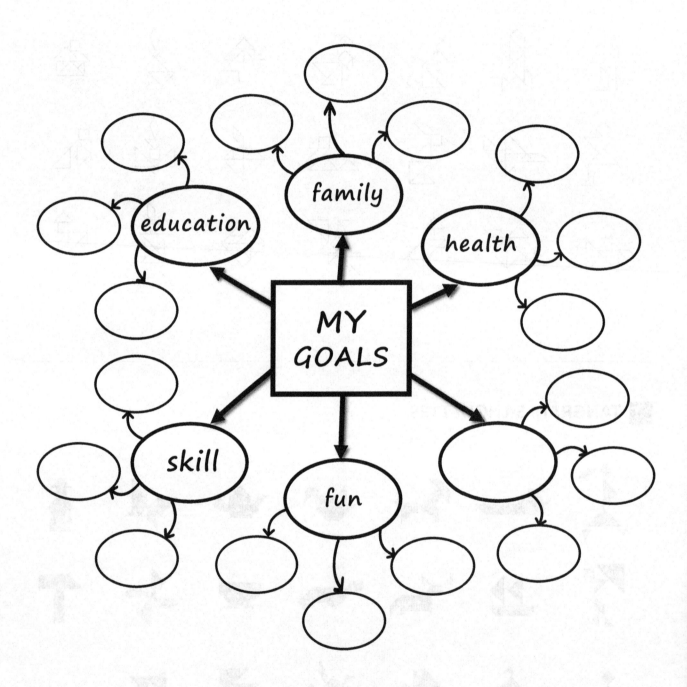

SMART GOALS

My goal: _____

SPECIFIC	Narrow down a larger desire into specific details. What is my target?	
MEASURABLE	What milestones can I set? How can I track my progress?	
ATTAINABLE	Is my goal realistic and reachable? How can I make it possible to achieve?	
RELEVANT	Why this goal? Why is this important to me?	
TIMED	Do I have a deadline? When do I want to reach my goal?	

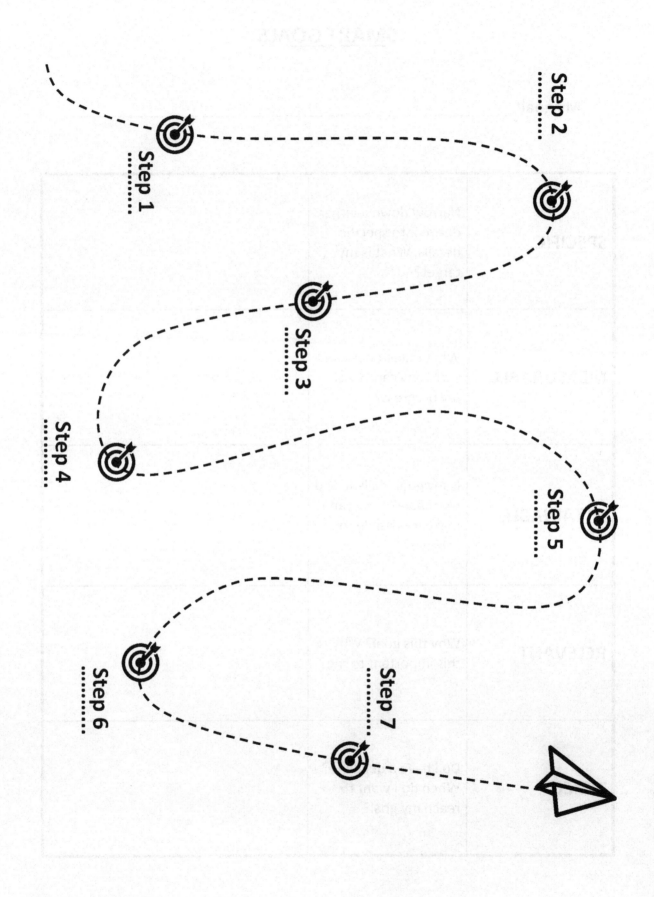

Step 1

Step 2

Step 3

Step 4

Step 5

Step 6

Step 7

Unit 9. Step by Step Map

(11) (3) (50) (21) (72) (33) (5) (91)

(93) (42) (61) (35) (86) (29) (18) (40)

(23)

(31) (9) (95) (14) (55) (78) (45) (58) (65)

(37) (2) (71) (99) (77) (39)

(4) (56) (83) (52)

(44) (25) (49) (20) (28)

(27) (70) (34) (98) (79) (68)

(84) (16) (89)

(19) (57) (7) (69) (41) (17)

(80) (53)

(38) (62) (73) (87) (24) (96)

(47) (30) (74) (97)

(22) (6) (90) (63) (48) (36)

(51) (32) (81) (59) (100) (43) (1)

(15) (60) (92) (76) (82)

(10) (75) (66) (88) (85) (46) (13) (67)

(64) (12) (94) (8) (54) (26)

Other Books by David Paris

50 Social Emotional Learning Lessons. Vol. 1

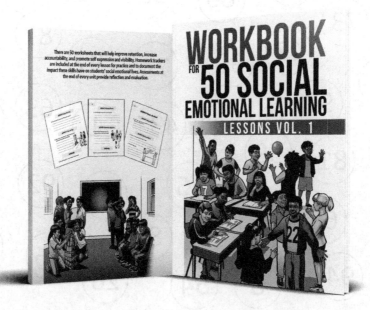

Workbook For 50 Social Emotional Learning Lessons Vol. 1

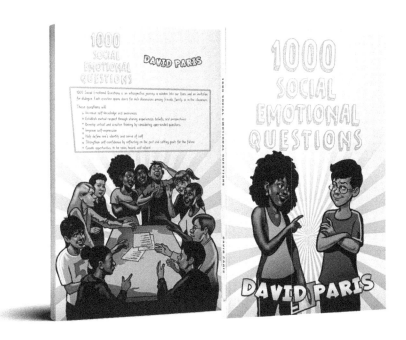

1000 Social Emotional Questions

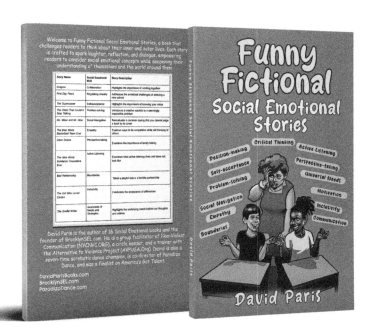

Funny Fictional Social Emotional Stories

Made in the USA
Las Vegas, NV
12 October 2024